T0129292

COACHING

Public Service Leaders

Seven Practices Good Leaders Master

John S. Lybarger, PhD, MCC

COACHING PUBLIC SERVICE LEADERS
SEVEN PRACTICES GOOD LEADERS MASTER

Copyright © 2019 John S. Lybarger, PhD, MCC.

All rights reserved. No part of this book may be used or reproduced by any means, graphic, electronic, or mechanical, including photocopying, recording, taping or by any information storage retrieval system without the written permission of the author except in the case of brief quotations embodied in critical articles and reviews.

iUniverse books may be ordered through booksellers or by contacting:

iUniverse
1663 Liberty Drive
Bloomington, IN 47403
www.iuniverse.com
1-800-Authors (1-800-288-4677)

Because of the dynamic nature of the internet, any web addresses or links contained in this book may have changed since publication and may no longer be valid. The views expressed in this work are solely those of the author and do not necessarily reflect the views of the publisher, and the publisher hereby disclaims any responsibility for them.

Any people depicted in stock imagery provided by Getty Images are models, and such images are being used for illustrative purposes only.
Certain stock imagery © Getty Images.

Author Credits: John S. Lybarger

ISBN: 978-1-5320-8000-5 (sc)
ISBN: 978-1-5320-8001-2 (e)

Library of Congress Control Number: 2019912253

Print information available on the last page.

iUniverse rev. date: 09/30/2019

Contents

CHAPTER 8

CHAPTER 9

Preface

Why do some public service employees love their work and remain actively engaged while others disengage and do the minimum to get by?

Why does fear so often win out over love? What does it take for love, belonging, and community to dispel fear, disengagement, and isolation?

Why are so many employees suffering from loneliness and isolation? What does it take to create togetherness and community?

What sustains those who are engaged and motivated to serve the public? What causes others to choose disengagement?

Why do some public service workers become successful leaders and some flounder? Is it possible for those who are floundering to flourish? What can they learn? How can they shift?

Why do some agencies have strong cultures of respect and trust while others are bogged down in a quagmire of disrespect, exclusion, and fear?

I have spent countless hours wrestling with these questions and talking with hundreds of public service workers about their opinions and perspectives. In this book, I explore what I have learned and what's needed to coach and grow successful public service leaders who inspire others to be actively engaged and thrive in a culture of love, respect, trust, inclusion, and belonging.

Over the past several years, I have noticed a significant pattern among federal agencies. They seem to struggle with the process of defining their leader competencies. Many do not adopt the executive core qualifications (ECQs) and leadership competencies model created by the US Office of Personnel Management (OPM) as a standard for all federal employees and agencies; instead, they create their own leader competency models. This lack of standardization has led to confusion and unnecessary complexity around what leader behaviors comprise successful public service, and I believe it is negatively influencing employee motivation and commitment.

Engagement, trust, accountability, courage, motivation, and commitment have become priority topics in most federal agencies. These are reflected in the 2017 OPM Viewpoint Survey (see appendix 6) and in many agency-specific climate surveys. Drawing upon my nearly thirty years of experience in executive coaching and leader development consulting, I have identified seven practices good leaders master that strengthen trust; inspire engagement; create accountability; encourage learning and mastery; assist with navigating complexity, chaos, and ambiguity; improve strategic thinking; and ensure mission execution. These seven practices are as follows:

1. Actionable trust
2. Authentic engagement
3. Aligned accountability
4. Adaptive learning and mastery
5. Aptly navigating complexity, chaos, and ambiguity
6. Adroitness at strategic thinking
7. Audacious pursuit of mission execution

Four enduring themes appear in the derailment research, as summarized by Ellen Van Velsor and Jean Brittain Leslie in their 1995 article "Why Executives Derail: Perspectives Across Time and Cultures" (16). These are as follows:

1. Problems with interpersonal relationships
2. Failure to meet business objectives
3. Failure to build and lead a team
4. Inability to change or adapt during a transition

In each chapter, these enduring themes are mapped to the practice that is covered. In appendix 2, you will find a comprehensive crosswalk: "Themes in Derailment Research" and "Seven Practices Good Leaders Master."

The seven leader practices function as the cornerstone of public service leader competencies. Regardless of which specific leader competencies are adopted, they will always be undergirded by these cornerstone practices. A practice is like a bucket. Inside the bucket are clusters of competencies that complement and support one another. When a leader develops mastery of a practice, he or she is fully competent in that practice.

The seven practices are not new. They are evident and prevalent among leaders in many agencies, and they have withstood the tests of time, politics, growth, and decline. Hundreds of books have been written, and thousands of studies have been conducted. This book is a guide to coaching public service leaders in the mastery of the seven practices. I have written it for both external coaches (who work with leaders within public service agencies) and internal coaches (public service leaders who provide coaching to their colleagues).

In September 2018, Dr. Jeff T. H. Pon, director of OPM, issued a Memorandum for Chief Human Capital Officers on Coaching in the Federal Government. In part, he wrote:

> Coaching is a critical tool as the Federal Government strives to develop a
> workforce that supports the effective and efficient mission achievement

and improved services to the American people. The benefits of coaching individuals and teams include higher engagement, retention, organizational performance and productivity; increased focus on mission and organization objectives; improved creativity, learning, and knowledge; and better relationships between people and departments. The field and practice of coaching is broad and contains many facets which will require more specific guidance. This memorandum and attached Frequently Asked Questions, provides guidance to Federal agencies as they plan, design, and implement coaching activities and programs. (See appendix 7 for full memorandum.)

Chapter 1 opens with Michael's first coaching conversation. He is a fictional character I have created to illustrate coaching conversations with public service employees. His story and all names, characters, and incidents portrayed in this book are fictitious. No identification with actual persons (living or deceased), places, buildings, or organizations is intended or should be inferred from the scripted conversations.

As you read through the book, you will get glimpses into Michael's coaching conversations. Following each conversation, you will learn about additional resources, assessments, and coaching tools you can use in your public service leadership coaching practice or in your role as a public service leader, coaching other public service leaders in your agency.

At the end of each of the first seven chapters, you will find a brief summary of the practice and key skills that were covered; a crosswalk mapping the practice to the ECQs and the twenty-eight leadership competencies; a resource list of suggested books, articles, and videos; and suggested assessments that provide deeper insight into the practice and skills.

Acknowledgments

Many friends, colleagues, and clients contributed to this book's creation. I am honored to have been a part of thousands of clients' lives during their leadership development journeys. Although Michael is a fictional character created specifically for this book and any resemblance to actual persons living or dead is purely coincidental and unintended by the author, his story reflects so many real-life clients' journeys in public service along the executive coaching path.

Many of my thoughts recorded here have evolved from my reading and interactions with authors, mentors, and colleagues I have studied with, listened to, and worked with throughout my career. Some of my favorite authors have also influenced my thinking, including Brené Brown, Jim Kouzes, Barry Posner, Barry Oshry, Peter Block, Richard Boyatzis, Travis Bradberry, Jean Greaves, Rick Brandon, William Bridges, Marcus Buckingham, Gary Chapman, Jim Collins, Stephen Covey, Steven M. R. Covey, Marshal Goldsmith, Daniel Goleman, Chip and Dan Heath, Rich Horwath, John Kotter, Gus Lee, Jim Loehr, Chris Musselwhite, Robert Quinn, Peter Senge, Simon Sinek, Julia Sloane, and Meg Wheatley.

Many colleagues and friends have contributed to my thinking as well. I would like to acknowledge Dr. Michael Black; Dr. David Burger; Mary Cooper; Cathy Daughenbaugh; Charles Fakes; Dr. Marrey Embers; Phil Evans; Dr. Steven Finney; Tim Flanagan; Dr. Cathy Gnam; Teressa Moore Griffin; Rev. Dr. Val Hastings, MCC; Kathy Helms; George Liscic; Dr. Marie Mactavish; Cheryl Martin; Amy Miller, MCC; Chuck Miller; Rev. Dr. Michael Noel; Julio Olalla, MCC; Dr. Tom Olschner; Dr. Richard Phillips; Marty Raphael, MCC; Cindy Wagner; Dr. Leanne Wells; and Dr. Julianne Wright.

I would also like to extend a special recognition and a word of appreciation to my colleagues who offered to review, edit, and give suggestions on my various manuscript drafts. These special people are Aimee Abdelrahman, Dr. Marrey Embers, Kathy Helms, Vicky Jordan, George Liscic, and Chuck Miller. Any errors in grammar, writing style, or references are mine alone.

CHAPTER 1

PRACTICE ONE:

Actionable Trust

I learned that trust truly does change everything. Once you create trust—genuine character- and competence-based trust—almost everything else falls into place.

—Stephen M. R. Covey, *Speed of Trust*

Michael began his first coaching session with me by sharing the following:

> Working with some of my colleagues is killing me! I feel like there are days when I'm wandering around in a toxic and poisonous culture without a hazmat suit or vaccinations. I used to love coming to work. Now I wake up some mornings with dread. My mind wanders, drifting from one scenario to another where I'm faced with resistance, disengagement, mistrust, and negativity.
>
> When I try to get people to work together, inevitably someone complains that they don't feel respected or are being mistreated. I've offered to meet with them and the person they are frustrated with, and they decline, saying it's not a safe place for them.
>
> When I attempted to use performance counseling and a performance improvement plan to turn things around, I felt undermined by human resources, legal, and my own supervisor when she told me I can't rate someone lower than acceptable or that I can't implement the disciplinary action that was cited in the performance improvement plan because the employee might file a complaint.
>
> It's not all bad. I have some great colleagues—senior leaders, peers, and subordinates who are still passionate about the mission. They are bright spots for me when I'm seeking a waypoint through the fog and mist of despair and disengagement. We try to support and encourage one another. I just feel like I should be doing something more. I hate feeling like a victim—the one who whines and

complains and does nothing to improve things. Sometimes it feels like quicksand, though, and I'm slowly sinking deeper into the bog.

Our budgets are being reduced. When people leave, we frequently lose the billets. Reorgs are the new norm—teams are combined, mission elements are integrated, mission priorities are realigned—and in the midst of these changes, people are floundering. I know I'm supposed to embrace and champion change. I struggle with doing that, though, when I no longer know who sits where or who does what in the new organization. It seems like we've lost sight of creating and maintaining sustainable systems, practices, policies, and procedures that transcend the reorgs and realignments. These are so desperately needed to stay focused on mission execution.

I've learned in some of my leadership classes that it's important to embrace curiosity. I know that this would help me be open to new, innovative, and creative approaches, and I struggle with wanting to hold on to how we've always done things. The tried and true gives me comfort, and it's been effective. The other practice I've been taught is to adopt a beginner's mind-set when I am trying new things. This sounds so easy, but it's really quite difficult!

The main obstacles I'm facing right now are navigating through the complexity, chaos, ambiguity, and constant change I face day in and day out. When I get overwhelmed by the complexity, I lose confidence in my decision-making. In the midst of chaos, I struggle with uncertainty and lack of direction. Growing up in the agency, I was constantly recognized and rewarded for my technical competence. I didn't struggle with ambiguity when I was engineering software, or designing a new system, or managing complex projects. Now, as a leader, I'm expected to make strategic decisions and cascade change-effort visions when the way forward is ambiguous and the future uncertain.

I don't know how to be strategic when tactical behaviors are the ones that get rewarded. When I try to be disciplined by applying quality decision-making and critical thinking to complex problems and mission requirements, my superiors get impatient. They want quick wins and immediate results. The ready-fire-aim approach is taxing. We fall into repetitive patterns of rework to fix unintended consequences and address missed mission requirements. My customers are losing faith and confidence. I want to rebuild trust in these relationships before it's too late.

If I could find a way to connect my agency's various strategies to day-to-day actions, I could enable and empower my teams to execute mission priorities more effectively. This would also help me identify their mission contributions and provide meaningful recognition.

I love our mission. My commitment to public service keeps me coming back even when it seems impossible at times to continue or the obstacles appear insurmountable. Each day, my resiliency fades, and my energy reserves deplete a little more. I want to find the courage to keep going, and I need to find ways to renew my sense of purpose and belonging with my agency and my team.

I came to you for coaching because I don't know where to begin. What can I do to improve my team's trust? How do I restore my first love for our mission so that I can remain engaged over the long haul? Is there a path forward amid the complexity, chaos, ambiguity, and constant change?

Michael's story is not unique. I have heard variations of it from thousands of public servants who want to make a difference and overcome similar obstacles and challenges. In my work as an executive coach and organization development consultant over the past twenty-seven years, I have had the honor and privilege of helping public servants navigate through the complexity, chaos, and change they face daily as they lead in a VUCA (volatile, uncertain, complex, and ambiguous) world.

Please listen in on the continuing coaching journey as I partner with Michael, cocreating an agenda and codesigning plans, actions, and goal-setting that will enable him to realize his personal leader development goals. Throughout Michael's coaching journey, I break away from the coaching conversation and provide additional information on the seven practices good leaders master, the specific skills needed to develop mastery of each practice, and suggested resources, including books, articles, videos, and assessments. This section is directed toward both external and internal coaches.

Let's return to the first meeting with Michael. I began our first coaching meeting with the following opening comments after Michael told me his story and why he was seeking coaching:

Michael, I'm honored that you've asked me to be your coach. I applaud your courage, your vulnerability, and your willingness to take a responsible risk by venturing into something new.

Your story is powerful and compelling. I can hear your passion and your pain. I see you're committed to doing the right thing, and you're torn by competing priorities and demands.

First, I want you to know that you aren't alone in this struggle. Your challenges aren't unique or new. Many have gone before you. Some have persevered and succeeded; others have floundered and failed. My commitment is to partner with you. Together, we'll create an agenda for change that meets your desired outcomes. Then we'll codesign a plan and specific actions to lead you toward your desired goals.

My role is to function as a guide and partner. I'll ask powerful questions, challenge your thinking, push you to expand your horizons, encourage you to embrace curiosity, and invite you to experiment with a beginner's mind.

Our relationship and the content of our conversations are confidential. I'll strive to honor you—your intelligence, creativity, competence, and humanity. I'll support your agenda, goals, actions, and desired outcomes. In turn, I'd like to request your commitment to the following ground rules for our coaching relationship:

- Begin and end our conversations on time.
- Be fully present and engaged in the conversation.
- Honor commitments to actions and practices between meetings.
- Assume self-responsibility for actions and outcomes.
- Make clear requests, offers, and promises to one another.

I'll make the same commitments to you.

Michael said he would make the same commitments to our coaching relationship and was grateful for the opportunity to participate in coaching. Our coaching conversation continued. I'll label the dialog with Coach (me) and Client (Michael) to make it easier for you to adapt this to your own needs.

Coach: As you reflect on what you've just shared with me and as you think about moving forward, what's most important to you to focus your attention toward first?

Client: Well, like I said, I'm not really sure where to begin. My biggest questions are:

- What can I do to improve my team's trust?
- How do I rekindle my love for our mission so that I can remain engaged over the long haul?
- Is there a path forward amid the complexity, chaos, ambiguity, and constant change?

Coach: Thinking about those three questions, which one has the strongest emotional pull for you?

Client: Wow, each one is compelling. Let me think about it a second … I'd have to say it's "How do I improve my team's trust?"

Coach: As you reflect on that question, what feelings do you have about it?

Client: I feel frustrated when my team members complain about feeling disrespected and mistreated and then refuse to talk about it. I feel discouraged when my attempts to resolve conflicts fail. At this point, I'm also feeling confused and uncertain about how to move forward.

Coach: What would it mean to you if you were able to accomplish improving your team's trust?

Client: It would mean that I had accomplished something very important and significant. Achieving improved team trust would inspire me to remain engaged and focused on the mission.

Coach: I invite you to think of a time when you were on a team with low trust and the leader was able to improve it. What actions did the leader take?

Client: I remember a few years ago, when I was a new branch chief, I had a supervisor who was the division chief. Her division had five branches. There was mistrust among the five of us branch chiefs. It seemed like all of us were looking out for our own needs without considering one another's needs within the division. Frequently we were in competition with one another over limited resources like budget, billets, and equipment. We didn't work like a team. Instead of collaborating and partnering, we operated in silos and withheld information.

Kathy was the division chief. She called the five of us in for a meeting. First, she asked us to each take a few minutes and reflect on several questions. She asked us to think about how we would describe the current trust climate on our team. Her questions were:

- What are we doing well?
- What could we do to improve?
- What could we consider doing less of?
- What do we need to consider doing more of?
- What do we need to consider stopping doing?
- What do we need to consider starting to do?
- What do we need to do differently?

These questions really challenged our thinking. We learned that we each wanted the same thing—deeper trust, more collaboration, less competition, and a shared vision of being one team with a shared mission. These seven questions led us to four questions that became the bones of each weekly team meeting, and they helped us stay on track to achieve our goals. As a team, we asked each member:

- What's the critical path?
- What are you working on?
- What are your obstacles?
- As a leadership team, how can we help you?

Coach: As you recall that leader's approach and the impact it had on repairing, extending, and strengthening trust on your team, what can you take away and apply to your present challenge of improving your team's trust?

Client: I can't believe I didn't remember how impactful those four questions were for our team! I guess I just took them for granted after using them regularly. I see myself I couldn't implement them with my current team, and I know I'm going to introduce them in next week's team meeting!

Coach: We are coming to the end of our time together today. It sounds like you have a plan for next week. I'll be looking forward to your progress report in our next meeting.

Michael's Action Steps

1. I will introduce the four questions to my team.
2. I will use the questions regularly in our meetings to help us track our goals and progress.

Three weeks later, Michael returned for his second coaching meeting.

Coach: Michael, it's great to see you! I'm looking forward to hearing about what's taken place since our first meeting. Where would you like to begin our conversation today?

Client: Thanks. I'd like to start with checking in on my progress regarding my goal from our first meeting. I planned to introduce the four questions in my next team meeting to help extend and strengthen trust among my eight team members.

To prepare for this strategy, I read a book: *The Speed of Trust: The One Thing That Changes Everything* by Stephen M. R. Covey (2018). Dr. Covey defined trust as "confidence born of the character and the competence of a person or an organization." He went on to say that character is defined by integrity, and intent and competence are defined by capabilities and results. Personal trust comes from credibility, and relationship trust comes from behaving in ways that inspire trust.

I knew I had to start with a dialogue about trust first. I opened the next team meeting by telling the group that I wanted to have a dialogue about team trust. Our meeting was scheduled for ninety minutes.

First, I asked each person to write down the words that came to mind when they thought about trust. Next, I asked, "What characteristics come to mind?" Then we shared our lists with the group. The items included the following:

- accountable
- dependable
- responsible
- brave
- predictable
- stewardship
- courageous
- reliable
- trustworthy

I asked the group, "On a scale of 1 to 10, with 1 being *absent* and 10 being *flourishing*, how would you rate the trust on our team?" They recorded their numbers on sticky notes. I collected them and posted them on the chart stand. Their eight ratings ranged from 3 to 7. It looked like this:

Question: How do you rate our team's trust?									
Scale: 1	2	3	4	5	6	7	8	9	10
Rating: 0	0	2	1	3	2	2	0	0	0

Next, I asked the group, "Using the same scale, where would you like to see the trust on our team?" They wrote down their numbers and I posted those too.

Question: How would you like to see the team's trust?										
Scale:	**1**	**2**	**3**	**4**	**5**	**6**	**7**	**8**	**9**	**10**
Rating:	0	0	2	1	3	2	2	0	0	0

Then I posed a question for dialogue: "What behaviors do we need to change to extend and strengthen trust on our team?

Our discussion was very helpful and enlightening. Some team members talked about how they felt unsupported by other team members. They made requests for future support. In response, other members made offers and promises of support. Everyone said they felt heard and understood at the end of the meeting. We reached consensus on team norms and behaviors. I closed the meeting by introducing the four questions as a framework for our ongoing team meetings, and this idea was unanimously accepted.

Coach: As you reflect on your progress, how are you feeling right now?

Client: I feel optimistic and hopeful. I feel confident my team will move forward and that we'll build trust in a deeper way with one another.

Coach: Is there anything else you want to consider or do regarding your team's trust?

Client: I'm pleased with the momentum, and I want to keep it going.

Coach: We have about twenty minutes left today. What's next on your agenda?

Client: The other two questions I had when we met last time were:
- How do I restore my love for our mission so that I can remain engaged over the long haul?
- Is there a path forward amid the complexity, chaos, ambiguity, and constant change?

Coach: Which one do you feel is most important to explore next?

Client: I think the first one is critical for me to look at next. I think my engagement varies day to day, and I want to get back to how I felt when I first entered public service. I loved our mission. I felt passionate about public service, and my motivation was high. I'd like to get that back. I'm just unsure how to do it.

Coach: As you think about returning to your first love for public service, what obstacles are in your way?

Client: First, I think I'm afraid of not being good enough. I mean, I worry that I won't be a good leader. I was really effective at managing my work as a technical expert and team member. I want to be just as good at leadership. Having the confidence that I know the right things to do and having the courage to do the right things even when it's hard are strong values. Connecting with others, fostering and building strong relationships, and creating a sense of belonging are really important to me.

Coach: You've identified several really important things. Which one is tugging at you the most right now?

Client: My fear seems to be the biggest obstacle. I want to explore that first.

Coach: When fear comes up for you, how do you experience it?

Client: I feel it in my body first. My breathing gets shallow, my palms get clammy, my muscles tense in my neck and shoulders, and my pulse quickens. I can't think about much else beyond getting away from the circumstances or trying to fight off the threats. Sometimes I just freeze and don't do anything for a minute or two.

I sometimes feel frightened that I'll do the wrong thing, or I get anxious that I will miss something critical and important. I feel overwhelmed by the confusion, and then I lose confidence in my abilities.

Coach: You seem to have a clear awareness of how fear manifests itself in your body. You're also able to identify and articulate the emotions that are triggered by your somatic responses.

Breathing is a key strategy for managing fear. I'd like to suggest that you read a book and experiment with the breathing technique it teaches. It's called *Three Deep Breaths: Finding Power and Purpose in a Stressed-Out World* by Thomas Crum (2006). How do you feel about trying that strategy?

Client: I'm curious, and I want to give it a try.

Coach: I think you'll discover that fear displaces belonging. When we remain in fear, we're unable to feel like we belong. Fear will sever connection every time. When we embrace belonging, fear is dispelled. Our breath is the key. We entered this world with our first breath, and we leave it with our last breath. In the interim, how we control breath influences how we live our lives. Embracing shallow breathing fuels fear, longing, rejection, isolation, and disconnection. Embracing deep breathing fuels love, belonging, acceptance, relationship, and connection.

We've reached the end of our time for today. As we wrap up, what actions are you committing to take between now and our next meeting?

Client: First, I'm going to get the book *Three Deep Breaths* and read it. Then I'll practice the breathing exercise. I used to journal, and I'm thinking that now might be a good time for me to put that back into practice. Journaling about my somatic and emotional reactions to fear might help me identify some patterns.

Coach: That sounds like a solid action plan. I'm looking forward to hearing about your progress in our next meeting.

Michael's Action Steps
1. Get the book *Three Deep Breaths* and read it.
2. Practice my breathing exercises.
3. Begin journaling again, focusing on my somatic and emotional reactions to fear, and look for patterns.

MASTERING ACTIONABLE TRUST

I'm not upset that you lied to me. I'm upset that from now on I can't believe you.
—Friedrich Nietzsche

Actionable trust is the practice of speaking and behaving in ways that extend trust to others, strengthen trust in relationships that need more, and rebuild trust in relationships where it's been broken. We master actionable trust by learning to extend, strengthen, and rebuild trust.

Relationships aren't possible without some degree of trust. We must believe that another person is trustworthy to some degree or we will not attempt to connect with that person in a meaningful way. Leaders extend, strengthen, and rebuild trust. A leader's trustworthy behaviors pave the way for constituents to choose to willingly follow. Followership is the act of choosing to extend trust toward a leader who has extended trust toward a potential follower. This exchange of extended and accepted trust creates a mutually trusting relationship.

Chalmers Brothers said in *Language and the Pursuit of Happiness: A New Foundation for Designing Your Life, Your Relationships, and Your Results* (2004) that when we make the declarations "I trust you" and "I don't trust you," we base them on three assessments or judgments that we have assigned to the individual. These are our assessments of sincerity, competency, and reliability or credibility. If our assessments of any of these three are negative, we will declare that we don't trust the person. Whenever we are distrusting, we can usually reflect on our assessments and discover that at least one of these three are missing.

When you are coaching clients around the practice of actionable trust, it's important to help them understand that trust is a behavior, not an emotion. We talk and act our way into trusting relationships, and we talk and act our way out of trusting relationships. You can best serve your coaching clients by guiding them through the process of clarifying what they want to say or do to extend trust, strengthen trust, or rebuild trust.

Let's begin by exploring the skill of extending trust.

EXTENDING TRUST

Extending trust when there are solid grounds to do so, when some evidence for trusting can be pointed to, is trusting with your eyes open and is considered to be prudent.
—Chalmers Brothers, *Language and the Pursuit of Happiness*

The skill of extending trust involves choosing to speak and act in ways that demonstrate our interest and willingness to offer trust to others. We may make a request of someone; this is an act of trusting that this individual is willing and able to honor our request. We can also accept a promise or an offer from someone. Our act of acceptance indicates we are trusting that the other person will follow through with this commitment to us.

We master the skill of extending trust by grounding our assessments of others' trustworthiness; risking responsibly when we make requests; accepting offers and promises from others; and speaking and behaving in courageous ways that communicate our boundaries, expectations, desires, and wishes. When you are coaching a client on actionable trust, extending trust frequently arises as a topic for exploration. It is necessary when relationships are new or when they shift and require more trust between the parties. Someone must decide to go first. Extending trust requires a belief in the other person—an assessment that this individual is worthy of your trust. It also requires responsible risk-taking, vulnerability, and courage.

Sometimes a good starting place in coaching is inviting the client to explore his or her assessment of whether or not the other person is worthy of trust. Some powerful questions to ground their assessments could include the following:

- How do you assess this person's sincerity?
- How do you assess this person's competence with the task at hand?
- How do you assess this person's reliability or credibility?
- How do you know this to be true?
- What have you seen this person do or heard this person say that has earned your trust?
- What else do you need to know before you extend trust?
- How will you know when you are ready to extend trust?
- What do you expect this other person to do when you extend trust?
- How have you done this successfully in the past?
- What can you apply to this situation from your past experiences?

After clients have grounded their assessment that another person is worthy of trust, you may explore willingness to engage in responsibly taking risks, practicing vulnerability, and demonstrating courage. Responsible risk-taking is about thinking through the potential risks and rewards of extending trust. It's about assessing the other person's trustworthiness. Extending trust requires us to be vulnerable. We need to make wise decisions about how much to share and how much to risk when we extend trust to others.

Demonstrating courage is about taking a stand for what you believe in. It's doing the right thing even when that's hard. Sometimes this takes the form of setting and maintaining clear boundaries. It takes courage to speak out about what you are comfortable with and what you are unwilling to accept from others. When we are clear about our boundaries, it's much easier for us to be compassionate, generous, forgiving, and patient. If we fail to set and maintain clear boundaries, we are at risk for feeling bitter and resentful when others cross our boundaries. Questions to consider including the following:

- How will you know you are ready?
- What boundaries do you need to support your risk-taking?
- What request do you want to make of this person?
- What offer are you making this person?
- What promises are you making to this person?
- How will you find your courage to extend trust to this person?
- Who else could support you in this process?

STRENGTHENING TRUST

> The decision to extend or not extend trust is always an issue of managing risk.
> —Stephen M. R. Covey, *The Speed of Trust*

The skill of strengthening trust is the act of wisely making requests, accepting offers or promises that add more responsibilities to the relationship, and increasing mutual dependencies upon one another's reliability and trustworthiness. It is about balancing risks and rewards in the context of a relationship.

We master the skill of strengthening trust by grounding our assessment that the other person has earned some degree of trust with us already and that we are willing to strengthen this existing trust by making additional requests or accepting additional offers or promises from someone. We may also strengthen another's trust in us by honoring our commitments to offers and promises we have made to them.

Sometimes clients will identify relationships in which trust exists and needs to be strengthened. This may happen when more responsibilities are added to the relationship or when mutual dependencies increase in scope or depth. This plays out in a variety of relationships like supervisors and direct reports; peer to peer; and customer service providers and customers. Of course, trust is also necessary between a coach and a client for the coaching relationship to work effectively for the client's purposes and agenda.

Strengthening trust works two ways. One is strengthening another's trust in you; the second is strengthening your trust in someone else. The following are some coaching questions to consider for strengthening another's trust in you:

- What did you say or do to extend trust in the beginning?
- What do you need to do more or less of to strengthen trust with this person?
- How do you know what the other person needs from you to strengthen trust?
- What are you willing to do to strengthen this other person's trust in you?

Consider the following questions for strengthening your trust in others:

- What did they say or do to extend trust in the beginning?
- What are you asking others to do or say to strengthen your trust in them?
- How will you know when you have strengthened trust with them?

REBUILDING TRUST

> We judge ourselves by our intentions and others by their behavior. This
> is why ... one of the fastest ways to restore trust is to make and keep
> commitments—even very small commitments—to ourselves and to others.
> —Stephen M. R. Covey, *The Speed of Trust*

The skill of rebuilding trust involves restoring broken trust. It may take the form of restoring others' trust in us when we have broken trust with them, or it may take the form of restoring our trust in someone who has broken trust with us. We master the skill of rebuilding trust by making and keeping our commitments. It's critical that we do what we say we are going to do; our talk must match our walk. Trust is rebuilt one action and one conversation at a time. When we rebuild trust wisely, we do so by exercising wisdom, discernment, good judgment, responsible risk-taking, and vulnerability.

Wisdom and discernment help us think through the potential risks and rewards of rebuilding trust with someone. If we naively seek to rebuild trust without wisely thinking about it first, we can set ourselves up for unnecessary pain, hurt, and suffering. Responsible risk-taking and vulnerability also both come into play when opportunities arise for rebuilding trust. Responsible risk-taking is about using wisdom and good judgment in determining how much trust to extend when starting out on the path of rebuilding broken trust.

Practicing vulnerability is about self-disclosure: deciding how much to share and when to share it during the rebuilding process. There are circumstances in our relationships that create opportunities for us to consider rebuilding trust. The following are some questions to consider when you are trying to rebuild someone's trust in you:

- What happened to break trust in this relationship?
- How can you find out what this person needs from you to rebuild trust?
- What are you willing to say or do to rebuild trust with this person?
- What promises or offers are you willing to make to this person to rebuild trust?

Consider the following questions when rebuilding your trust in someone else:

- What happened to cause you to lose trust in this person?
- What do you need this person to say or do to rebuild trust with you?
- How will you know that trust has been rebuilt?
- What risks are you willing to take with this person to rebuild trust?
- What boundaries do you need to put into place to make this process safe for you?
- What requests do you have for this person to help you rebuild your trust?

EXECUTIVE DERAILMENT FACTORS

The Center for Creative Leadership has been studying executive derailment factors for over twenty-five years. They define a derailed executive as "one who, having reached a general manager level, finds that there is little chance of future advancement due to a misfit between job requirements and personal skills" (Van Velsor and Leslie 1995). Over the years, the following four enduring themes have emerged in global studies of executive derailment:

1. Problems with interpersonal relationships
2. Failure to meet business objectives
3. Failure to build and lead a team
4. Inability to change or adapt during a transition

Problems with Interpersonal Relationships

According to Van Velsor and Leslie (1995), "Managers who have problems with interpersonal relationships are those who are successful early in their careers generally because they are good at what is often referred to as task-based leadership. When presented with a higher-level job that requires a more relationship-oriented leadership style, however, they have a difficult time." Additional characteristics include being overly critical, using others to further one's own ambitions, a penchant toward authoritarianism (ruling by fear or acting dictatorial), and an unwillingness to communicate or a preference for operating on a solitary basis.

Failure to Meet Business Objectives

In every derailment study, derailed managers had a track record of performance that contributed to their early career success. This was due, in part, to functioning in jobs that required technical skills or making and executing decisions independently in a stable environment. However, when conditions changed and new skills and methods of working with others were needed, these same managers faced productivity problems. Characteristics of a failure to meet business objectives include lack of follow-through on promises, being overly ambitious, inability to deliver results (seen as a betrayal of trust), and unjustified self-promotion (Van Velsor and Leslie 1995).

Failure to Build and Lead a Team

Derailment factors are closely intertwined. For example, the inability to build and lead a team may lead to a failure to meet business objectives. It may also have been a function of the task versus relationship personality orientation discussed under problems with interpersonal relationships. Characteristics of the inability to build and lead a team include challenges employing a participative leadership style, being too assertive, or demonstrating too much initiative (Van Velsor and Leslie, 1995).

Inability to Change or Adapt During a Transition

This fourth theme has multiple dimensions, including failure to adapt to a new boss with a different style; overdependence on a single skill; failure to acquire new skills; inability to adapt to new job demands, new culture, or market changes; and being unable or unwilling to learn from or apply feedback. In the most recent studies, significant importance has been placed on being able to change or develop in job, culture, or organization transition periods and being able to adapt one's thinking to marketplace changes (Van Velsor and Leslie 1995).

OPM Derailment Factors

The US Office of Personnel Management (OPM), Human Capital Management Leadership, has identified thirteen derailers that are related to their executive core qualifications, leadership competencies, organizational impact, and overall effectiveness. The OPM Leadership 360 assessment measures these thirteen behaviors. When these thirteen behaviors are not present, or a leader minimally demonstrates them, they are considered derailers. They are as follows:

Fundamental Competencies
Competency: Interpersonal Skills
1. Treats others with courtesy and respect.
Competency: Continual Learning
2. Learns from mistakes.

ECQ: Leading Change
Competency: Flexibility
3. Adapts to organizational change.
4. Is open to new ideas and opinions from others.

ECQ: Leading People
Competency: Conflict Management
5. Manages and resolves conflicts effectively.
Competency: Leveraging Diversity
6. Respects cultural, religious, gender, and racial differences.
Competency: Team Building
7. Inspires pride and team spirit among team members.
8. Builds teams of appropriate size and structure to accomplish work goals.

ECQ: Results Driven
Competency: Accountability
9. Achieves results within set time frames.
Competency: Decisiveness
10. Makes sound and timely decisions.

Organizational Impact
(This category of questions is not asked of the individual taking the OPM Leadership 360 assessment, only the raters are asked to assess the individual taking the assessment).
11. Recognizes personal strengths and weaknesses.
12. Leads without micromanaging.

Overall Effectiveness

13. Overall, how effective would this person be leading a different functional or technical area?

SELF-AWARENESS:
THE FOUNDATION OF DERAILMENT PREVENTION

Self-awareness is the primary skill that influences the other three skills that comprise emotional intelligence. Researchers (Goleman 1995, 1998; Goleman and Boyatzis 2002; Bradberry 2009; Stein 2011) have defined emotional intelligence as being comprised of self-awareness, self-regulation, social awareness, and relationship management. They have concluded that self-awareness is the cornerstone of emotional intelligence. Without it, the other skills that combine with it to form emotional intelligence cannot be fully developed. Deficits in emotional self-awareness impair self-regulation, social awareness, and relationship-management skills.

Self-awareness is also the foundation of derailment prevention. All derailment themes and behaviors can be traced back to a lack of or underdeveloped self-awareness. Problems with interpersonal relationships stem from deficiencies in emotional intelligence. When leaders lack self-awareness, they have a restricted capacity to consciously be aware of how what they say and do impacts others. These blind spots make it difficult for leaders to regulate their emotional expression and behaviors, and lack of self-regulation can result in impulsive outbursts and behaviors that impair interpersonal relationships. When leaders lack the ability to effectively assess what they are feeling and doing; make conscious, informed choices about their actions; and accurately read social situations to understand their impact, they suffer from problems with interpersonal relationships. This, in turn, makes it difficult for them to effectively manage interpersonal relationships.

Failure to meet business objectives stems from deficiencies in emotional intelligence and its four skills. When a betrayal of trust occurs, direct reports perform poorly, follow-through and hard workers lacking, or the leader is too ambitious, underdeveloped emotional intelligence is again at the core. First, leaders need to be self-aware and able to assess their part in it. Second, they need the skill to articulate their emotions and effectively regulate words and deeds. Third, they need to be skillful at accurately reading social cues and using this data to effectively manage interpersonal relationships. These steps are essential to rebuilding trust, engaging disengaged or underperforming employees, and holding oneself and others fully accountable for business objectives.

Problems with inability to build and lead a team—such as circumstances where staffing is ineffective, subordinates are being mismanaged, or difficulties are arising with molding a staff or building and leading a team—all stem from deficiencies in emotional intelligence and its four skills. When a leader has insufficient self-awareness, self-regulation, social awareness, and relationship-management skills, he or she will struggle with fostering engagement and building and leading teams effectively.

Problems with an inability to change or adapt during a transition can show up as an inability to adapt to a boss with a different style, an inability to adapt to a culture, strategic differences with management, difficulty making strategic decisions, an inability to develop or adapt, and conflict with upper management. When a leader has insufficient self-awareness, self-regulation, social awareness, and relationship-management skills, he or she will struggle with championing or leading change and adapting to new circumstances and situations during times of transition. With insufficient self-awareness, leaders will struggle with flexing and adapting to relationships with superiors and shifts in culture following downsizings, realignments, reorganizations, and mergers. When leaders don't have sufficient social awareness and relationship-management skills, they will struggle with practicing dialogue, and this will impair their strategic decision-making and conflict management skills.

ACTIONABLE TRUST DERAILERS

Three enduring themes in derailment research by Ellen Van Velsor and Jean Brittain Leslie (1995) apply to actionable trust:

1. **Problems with interpersonal relationships**
   When leaders fail to extend or strengthen trust or when they betray trust, they create interpersonal relationship problems. When trust is withheld or is weak or broken, conflict escalates, people are driven into isolation and withdrawal, and employees' attention and efforts are diverted from critical mission-area functions and requirements.

2. **Failure to meet business objectives**
   When direct reports feel they have experienced a betrayal of trust by peers or superiors, they can easily be distracted from meeting business objectives. Their energies are directed at self-preservation instead of mission execution. Efforts to rebuild trust help with redirecting efforts toward critical mission areas.

3. **Inability to change or adapt during a transition**
   When leaders have conflict with their upper management, they may struggle with an inability to change or adapt during a transition. They may struggle with trusting their upper management's sincerity, competence, reliability, or credibility.

OPM's Fundamental Competencies cluster has one competency, interpersonal skills, that has one derailer that applies to practice one:

1. **Treats others with courtesy and respect.**

   Leaders who fail to treat others with courtesy and respect risk derailment due to problems with interpersonal relationships. These behaviors may be unintended and a consequence of being uninformed. Coaching could focus on uncovering hidden assumptions, identifying unconscious bias, and increasing awareness around culture, courtesy, and respect expectations.

When you are coaching a leader who may be at risk for derailment around problems with interpersonal relationships, failure to meet business objectives, an inability to change or adapt during a transition, or a failure to treat others with courtesy and respect, it may be helpful to reference the research and link it to developing mastery in practice one by strengthening the three supporting skills: extending trust, strengthening trust, and rebuilding trust.

Use the themes and behaviors checklist to identify potential derailment themes and behaviors you would like to work on in coaching. Check off those that have been a challenge or a source of tension, or those that may benefit from further reflection and exploration.

Practice One: Actionable Trust	Derailment Themes*	Derailment Behaviors*
❏ Extend trust ❏ Strengthen trust ❏ Rebuild trust	❏ Problems with interpersonal relationships ❏ Failure to meet business objectives ❏ Inability to change or adapt during a transition	❏ Betrayal of trust ❏ Does not lead without micromanaging ❏ Conflict with upper management

*Derailment Themes adapted from *Themes in Derailment Research* (Van Velsor and Leslie 1995, Table 1). Derailment Behaviors adapted from *Themes in Derailment Research* (Van Velsor and Leslie 1995), OPM Leadership 360.

Chapter Summary

Actionable trust is the practice of speaking and behaving in ways that extend trust to others, strengthen trust in relationships that need more, and work to rebuild trust in relationships where it's been broken. The following are actionable trust skills:

- **Extending trust**—the act of choosing to speak and act in ways that demonstrate our interest and willingness to offer trust to others. For example, making a request of someone is an act of trusting that they are willing and able to honor our request. We can also accept a promise or an offer from someone. Our act of acceptance indicates we are trusting that they will follow through with their commitment to us.

- **Strengthening trust**—the act of wisely making requests or accepting offers or promises from someone that add more responsibilities to the relationship and increase mutual dependencies upon one another's reliability and trustworthiness. It is about balancing risks and rewards.

- **Rebuilding trust**—the act of restoring broken trust. It may take the form of restoring someone else's trust in us when we have broken trust with them, or it may take the form of restoring our trust in someone who has broken trust with us.

Crosswalk: OPM ECQs and Competencies and Practice One: Actionable Trust

OPM ECQs and Competencies*	Practice One: Actionable Trust
Fundamental Competencies	
Integrity/Honesty: Behaves in an honest, fair, and ethical manner. Shows consistency in words and actions. Models high standards of ethics.	• extending trust • strengthening trust • rebuilding trust
ECQ: Leading People This core qualification involves the ability to lead people toward meeting the organization's vision, mission, and goals. Inherent to this ECQ is the ability to provide an inclusive workplace that fosters the development of others, facilitates cooperation and teamwork, and supports constructive resolution of conflicts.	
Conflict Management: Encourages creative tension and differences of opinions. Anticipates and takes steps to prevent counter-productive confrontations. Manages and resolves conflicts and disagreements in a constructive manner.	• extending trust • strengthening trust • rebuilding trust
ECQ: Results Driven This core qualification involves the ability to meet organizational goals and customer expectations. Inherent to this ECQ is the ability to make decisions that produce high-quality results by applying technical knowledge, analyzing problems, and calculating risks.	
Technical Credibility: Understands and appropriately applies principles, procedures, requirements, regulations, and policies related to specialized expertise.	• extending trust • strengthening trust • rebuilding trust

*OPM ECQs and Competencies quoted from OPM Executive Core Qualifications, https://www.opm.gov/policy-data-oversight/senior-executive-service/executive-core-qualifications/.

RESOURCES

Books, Articles, Videos

Atkins, Andy. 2012. "How Leaders Build Trust." *Fast Company*, August 7. http://www.fastcompany.com/3000204/how-leaders-build-trust.

Brothers, Chalmers. 2004. *Language and the Pursuit of Happiness: A New Foundation for Designing Your Life, Your Relationships, and Your Results*. Naples, Florida: New Possibilities Press.

Covey, Stephen M. R. 2018. *The Speed of Trust: The One Thing That Changes Everything*. New York: Free Press.

Crum, Thomas. 2006. *Three Deep Breaths: Finding Power and Purpose in a Stressed-Out World*. San Francisco: Barrett Koehler Publications, Inc.

Edmondson, Amy C. 2004. "Psychological Safety, Trust, and Learning in Organizations: A Group-Level Lens." In *Trust and Distrust in Organizations*, edited by Roderick Kramer and Karen Cook. New York: Russell Sage Foundation.

Frei, Frances. 2018. "How to Build (and Rebuild) Trust." TED2018, April. https://www.ted.com/talks/frances_frei_how_to_build_and_rebuild_trust?language=en.

Glaser, Judith. 2014. *Conversational Intelligence: How Great Leaders Build Trust and Get Extraordinary Results*. Milton Park, Abington, Oxon, OX: Bibliomotion.inc.

Goleman, D., R. Boyatzis, and A. McKee. (2002). *Primal Leadership. Realizing the Power of Emotional Intelligence*. Boston: Harvard Business School Publishing.

_____. (1995). *Emotional Intelligence: Why It Can Matter More Than IQ*. New York: Bantam Doubleday Dell Publishing Group.

_____. (1998). *Working with Emotional Intelligence*. New York, NY: Bantam.

Horsager, David. 2009. *The Trust Edge: How Top Leaders Gain Faster Results, Deeper Relationships, and a Stronger Bottom Line*. New York: Free Press/Simon & Schuster.

Hurley, Robert F. 2006. "The Decision to Trust." *Harvard Business Review*, September.

Lencioni, Patrick. 2002. *The Five Dysfunctions of a Team: A Leadership Fable*. San Francisco: Jossey-Bass.

Patterson, Kerry, Joseph Grenny, Ron McMillan, and Al Switzler. 2002. *Crucial Confrontations: Tools for Resolving Broken Promises, Violated Expectations, and Bad Behavior*. New York: McGraw-Hill.

Sinek, Simon. 2011. "First Why and Then Trust." TEDxMaastricht. https://www.youtube.com/watch?v=4VdO7LuoBzM.

Van Velsor, Ellen, and Jean Brittain Leslie. 1995. "Why Executives Derail: Perspectives across Time and Cultures." *Academy of Management Executive* 9 (4): 62–72.

Recommended Assessments

Five Behaviors of a Cohesive Team® (Inscape Publishing)

A team assessment to measure a team's five behaviors that contribute to building cohesive teams: trust one another, engage in conflict around ideas, commit to decisions, hold one another accountable, and focus on achieving collective results.

OPM Leadership 360 (US Office of Personnel Management)

Measures the fundamental competencies and five executive core qualifications (ECQs), including the twenty-two supporting leadership competencies.

Political Savvy Assessment® (Brandon Partners)

Measures the following strategies:
- **character strategies**—personal integrity, performance integrity
- **awareness strategies**—knows the corporate buzz, studies politics, savvy attitudes
- **proactive strategies**—manages perceptions, essential networking, balanced self-promotion, enhances power image, savvy communication, ethical lobbying
- **protective strategies**—detects deception, handles sabotage

CHAPTER 2

PRACTICE TWO:

Authentic Engagement

Vulnerability is the birthplace of love, joy, trust, intimacy, courage—everything that brings meaning to our life.

—Brené Brown, *Braving the Wilderness*

Four weeks later, Michael returned for his third coaching meeting. He started the conversation with a check-in on his action-plan progress from our last meeting.

> Client: First, I got the book *Three Deep Breaths* (Crum 2006) and read it. I've been practicing the three deep breaths breathing exercise at least twice daily, and I'm noticing changes. I also began journaling again, and it's been helpful. I've been able to capture my somatic and emotional reactions to fear on several occasions this past month.
>
> Coach: It sounds like you've made great progress since our last meeting. What would you like to start with during our coaching conversation today?
>
> Client: Like I said in our last meeting, I think I'm afraid of not being good enough. I
>
> as a technical expert and team member. I want to be just as good at leadership.
>
> Coach: Can you tell me about a recent time when these feelings came up for you?
>
> Client: Sure. Just a few days ago, my technical lead missed a critical deadline on a special project. He's always been reliable and responsible. I was surprised when he dropped the ball on this—and I know he knew how important the project was to our senior leadership. I was afraid to confront him because I knew he was probably already beating himself up for it anyway. Holding him accountable and figuring out how to ensure it doesn't repeat was important to me, and I was afraid to talk to him.
>
> Coach: What did you fear might happen if you talked to him?

Client: I didn't want to alienate him. If I confronted him, he might have pulled back or dropped his productivity levels.

Coach: If you don't talk with him about it, what could happen?

Client: Well, I think he knows how serious it was and how badly it hurt our division. I want to think he will do whatever it takes to keep anything like this from happening again. If I don't talk with him, though, I can't know for sure that he does understand the full impact of his behavior, and I won't know that he has a viable plan in place to avoid a repeat in the future.

Coach: As you think of that possible scenario, how are you feeling about your options?

Client: I need to know that he knows the impact he had on our team by missing the deadline, and I need to know he has a viable plan in place to avoid missing future deadlines.

Coach: What's your next step?

Client: I'll make time to discuss it with him tomorrow.

Coach: How will you manage your fear about the conversation and his possible reactions?

Client: I've learned from practicing my breathing that when I'm feeling anxious or afraid, I can shift my emotions by shifting my breathing. It's really amazing how breathing deeply and centering my thoughts for just a few minutes changes me in so many ways! I feel calmer and more confident. My thoughts are clearer in the moment. A few minutes before my meeting with him, I'm going to practice my breathing and get myself centered.

Coach: You have learned to practice your breathing quite effectively. I can see the progress you've made and the benefits you are reaping. Congratulations! Your efforts have been quite effective. You said you've been journaling again. Can you recall any reflections from your journaling that cause you to question your leadership effectiveness?

Client: Yes. I saw a pattern. Whenever I'm faced with conflict or difficult conversations, I withdraw. Facing it head-on is rarely my first choice. Looking for ways to convince myself it's not that serious is usually first on my agenda.

I noticed that when I avoid conflict or difficult conversations, the conflict escalates and the tension in my relationship builds. When I eventually face the conflict or hold the conversation, I have to work harder, and the emotions are usually intensified. When I face the conflict earlier and hold difficult conversations promptly, I don't have to work as hard, and the emotions rarely escalate as much as they do when I delay taking any action.

Coach: How has seeing these patterns influenced your behavior and your fear of not being a good-enough leader?

Client: I see that I'm able to resolve conflict when I face it. My employees have told me they appreciate my empathy and my direct communication. I also see that when I choose to hold difficult conversations, I'm able to express my requests, clarify my expectations, and genuinely listen to the other person as we dialogue about how to move forward. Seeing these patterns and getting this feedback motivates me to be more consistent in stepping into conflict resolution sooner and holding difficult conversations much more promptly when a need arises. And practicing my breathing could really help me prepare for both of these situations.

Coach: You've learned a lot in a short period of time. I see you demonstrating courage and responsible risk-taking as you stretch yourself and step into difficult and challenging circumstances. I believe you'll find yourself feeling more confident in your leadership abilities as you continue to experiment with these new behaviors by facing your fears. You'll see your team grow in trust and in unity. Your example will empower them to manage conflict and hold difficult conversations too. These things will nurture a sense of purpose and belonging among your team members. Remember it's human nature to want to be a part of something bigger than ourselves. You're guiding your team in ways that will foster engagement, connection, purpose, and belonging.

We're nearing the end of our time today. What actions are you willing to commit to in the coming weeks?

Client: I'm going to choose to step in and resolve conflicts as soon as they arise, and I'm going to hold difficult conversations promptly when circumstances make it necessary. And I'm going to schedule a meeting for tomorrow with my tech lead to discuss the missed project deadline, its impact on the team, and his plan to avoid this happening in the future.

Michael's Action Steps

1. Step in and resolve conflicts as they arise.
2. Hold difficult conversations promptly.
3. Schedule a meeting with my tech lead and discuss the missed project deadline. Talk about how this impacted the team and ask him for a plan to avoid future occurrences.

MASTERING AUTHENTIC ENGAGEMENT

The greatest thing you'll ever learn is just to love and be loved in return.
—Eden Ahbez

Authentic engagement is the practice of genuinely and authentically connecting with others. It's about dispelling fear and loving one another. It's about creating and fostering a sense of belonging. It's the belief that we are a part of something bigger than ourselves, and it's about cultivating the courage to be vulnerable—to be open to joy, compassion, meaning, and purpose. We master authentic engagement by learning to dispel fear, foster belonging, and cultivate courage.

When I am coaching clients, they often want to work on engagement. They may choose to focus on increasing their personal engagement, or they may want to explore ways to improve the engagement of others around them.

DISPELLING FEAR

> Everything you want is on the other side of fear.
> —Jack Canfield

The skill of dispelling fear involves learning to react unconsciously and impulsively less frequently and to respond consciously and intentionally more frequently to strong emotions. It's the act of shifting one's emotional and physiological states from fear and stress to love and relaxation. We master the ability to dispel fear by learning to regulate our breathing. Deep breaths shift our neurochemistry and change our physiology.

When we are in the midst of feeling afraid, we often find ourselves in the fight-flight-freeze state. We quickly attempt to assess threats or danger and decide whether to fight back, flee the situation, or shut down and become immobilized. By breathing deeply, we inhibit the fight-flight-freeze reaction. Our physiology shifts again, and we are able to stop, think, and reflect before taking action. We move from impulsively reacting to fear to intentionally responding to our circumstances.

> Fear is the path to the Dark Side. Fear leads to anger,
> anger leads to hate, hate leads to suffering.
> —Yoda

Fear is a powerful primary emotion. It manifests itself in a wide variety of emotions and mental states. When we experience fear, it may be a fear of physical hurt or a fear of emotional hurt. Fear has a broad range of expression. For example, we may fear feeling or being any number of the following:

• attacked	• unsuccessful	• judged
• betrayed	• humiliated	• rejected
• embarrassed	• incompetent	• shamed

Fearful feelings lead to a variety of states of being, including alienation, disconnection, disengagement, isolation, marginalization, retaliation, and withdrawal.

Dispelling fear is a learnable skill. First, we need to understand fear as an emotion and as a biochemical reaction that we experience physically as well as emotionally. We all have emotions. We can't control what we feel. We can learn how to regulate our reactions and our responses to our emotions.

Recent studies in brain chemistry have validated that we experience our emotions first in reaction to an event. This is a precognitive process. We feel our emotions before we can think about them. In routine circumstances, someone says or does something, and then we react with comfortable emotions. Immediately, we associate their words or actions with a past event. This helps us make meaning out of the circumstances or make up a story about it. Next, we use our prefrontal cortex—our thinking brain—to make choices about how to respond. Our thinking brain helps us think critically, make quality decisions, and engage in effective problem-solving and planning.

Stress and anxiety increase when we face fear. When someone says something or does something that frightens, scares, or threatens us, we react with fear. This is often referred to as the fight, flight, or freeze response. Amid fearful, stressful circumstances, our neurochemistry changes. We have several hormones and neurotransmitters that regulate our bodily functions. Norepinephrine and epinephrine are two that flood our system when we are stressed. They stimulate our central nervous system.

Norepinephrine and epinephrine are both hormones, but they work differently. Epinephrine works on the major arteries; the heart and lungs; and the arteries in our skeletal muscles. It increases blood sugar levels, heart rate, and heart contractions, and it relaxes smooth muscles in the airways to make breathing easier. Norepinephrine only works on the arteries. It has similar effects to epinephrine as described above, and it also narrows blood vessels, which increases blood pressure.

Whenever we are afraid, we lose some of our ability to engage our thinking brain or our prefrontal cortex. Our focus shifts to survival, and we have limited abilities to think critically, objectively, strategically, or rationally. The more severe the perceived threat, the stronger our survival response is to counteract it, and the more impairment we experience in the ability to think critically.

Reactions are impulsive statements and actions that we engage in without forethought. Responses are thoughtful statements and actions. We are capable of responding only after we've had time to reflect, consider, and think through our options. We can usually do this when we are calm. Since fear can cause us to react impulsively, it's important to learn how to react less, respond more, and avoid making impulsive decisions and taking impulsive actions. Before we can make this shift from reacting to responding, we must first learn to dispel fear.

As Michael learned in his coaching, breath is a critical factor in dispelling fear. When we are afraid, our breathing becomes shallow. Shallow breathing increases our heart rate and elevates our blood pressure. Deep abdominal breathing decreases our heart rate and lowers our blood pressure. It also enhances full oxygen exchange by increasing the inspiration of oxygen and the expiration of carbon monoxide.

By intentionally shifting our breathing from fast and shallow to slow and deep, we shift our body's neurochemistry. We increase oxygen and blood circulation throughout our body, and we experience a sense of calm and relaxation. When we are calm and relaxed, we can engage our prefrontal cortex and use our critical, rational thinking skills. This helps us shift from a threat-survival mode to a purposeful, intentional mode—from reacting to responding.

The following are questions to consider when coaching someone to dispel fear:

- How is fear serving you?
- What would it mean to you to dispel your fear?
- What are you fearful of right now?
- Where do you feel fear in your body?
- Imagine you could give voice to your fear. What would it say to you?
- As you think about your fear, what is it telling you that you need?
- After you practice taking three deep breaths, what do you notice that's different with your body? With your emotions?

FOSTERING BELONGING

True belonging is the spiritual practice of believing in and belonging to yourself so deeply that you can share your most authentic self with the world and find sacredness in both being a part of something and standing alone in the wilderness. True belonging doesn't require you to change who you are; it requires you to be who you are ... We want true belonging, but it takes tremendous courage to knowingly walk into hard moments.
—Brené Brown, *Braving the Wilderness*

The skill of fostering belonging involves being who you are. It means deeply believing in yourself and courageously sharing your authentic self with others. You discover sacredness in both taking a stand when facing the unknown alone and becoming a part of something bigger than yourself in connection with others who share a belief in something meaningful and purposeful.

We master the ability to foster belonging by dispelling fear and embracing love. Love creates feelings of acceptance, belonging, connection, and behaviors like community, engagement, fellowship, forgiveness, and relationship. Learning to foster belonging is the starting place for clients who want to master authentic engagement. It's part of our human nature to want to belong. When we are isolated and alone, we long for connection. When we feel marginalized or excluded, we long for acceptance and inclusion.

BELONGING

You are the place where I stand on the day when my feet are sore.
—Pádraig ó Tuama, *Belonging Creates and Undoes Us*

Belonging is an emotional response we experience when we feel loved. When we are loved, we feel like we belong. Before we can unconditionally accept love from someone else, we must first learn to practice self-love. Self-love is self-compassion; it's a secure sense of self-acceptance. Loving ourselves unconditionally, just as we are, frees us to extend our love to others in the same way.

SELF-LOVE

> I don't trust people who don't love themselves and tell me, "I love you." ... There is an African saying which is: Be careful when a naked person offers you a shirt.
> —Maya Angelou

Coaching clients often struggle with the concept and practice of self-love. When developing and nurturing self-love is chosen by the client as part of the coaching agenda, it's important that the coach partners with the client in the exploration of personally assessing and deepening that individual's capacity for self-love.

Coaches can partner with their clients to explore a variety of actions that can help develop and nurture self-love. These include the following:

- creating and meditating on positive self-affirmations
- clarifying personal values and identifying how they show up in words and deeds
- writing a personal vision statement
- discovering what the client believes in—his or her personal "why?"
- identifying patterns in negative self-talk and reframing them into positive self-talk
- identifying personal strengths
- practicing gratitude

LOVE IS A PRIMARY EMOTION

Love, like fear, is a primary emotion. We can't control experiencing either one; however, we can learn to manage and regulate our actions in response to feeling love or fear. Fear and love cannot coexist in the same person or in a relationship. Fear dispels love; love dispels fear. Fostering belonging involves dispelling fear and nurturing love.

Dictionary.com defines *love* as "a profoundly tender, passionate affection for another person; a feeling of warm personal attachment or deep affection, as for a parent, child, or friend." The ancient Greeks had six different words for love (Krznaric 2013).

- *eros*—sexual passion and desire
- *philia*—a deep comradery or friendship that grows between warriors fighting alongside one another, showing loyalty, sacrifice, and sharing emotions
- *ludus*—playful love, like affection among children, bantering and laughing with friends, or singing and dancing
- *agape*—love for everyone; a selfless love or universal loving kindness
- *pragma*—longstanding love; the mature, deep, realistic love found between couples with a long relationship history. Pragma is about compromising, patience, and tolerance to strengthen a relationship. It's about making an effort to express love instead of only seeking to receive it.

- *philautia*—self-love. Philautia has two forms. Narcissism is self-obsessed and focused on personal fortune and fame. Self-compassion is a secure sense of self and the belief that you have plenty of love to extend to others.

As we can see from the variety of words that define love, it can have a broad range of expression in the workplace. When we feel loved, we feel or experience several emotions, including the following:

• acceptance	• generosity	• intimacy
• affirmation	• grace	• validation
• compassion	• inclusion	• vulnerability

Jim Kouzes and Barry Pozner, in *The Leadership Challenge*, explain that leadership can be summed up in one word: *relationship*. Leadership is about relationships. People don't care what you know; they care that you care. If people believe you care about them, they are much more likely to willingly follow your lead. It's really about loving your followers and leading them.

DIALOGUE

Dialogue is a communication tool that fosters belonging. It is useful in coaching, and it's useful in any size group conversation in any setting. Dialogue is a form of communication between two or more people that creates shared understanding across diverse perspectives; surfaces hidden assumptions; and deepens awareness and understanding of complex ideas, challenges, and options. It's a unique form of communication.

Dialogue brings people together, unifying them around a common purpose. When we are united around a purpose we believe in, we sense that we are a part of something bigger than ourselves. We feel like we belong—like we are united with others who share a common vision, mission, and purpose. Dialogue is not about any of the following:

• debating	• negotiating
• arguing	• converting
• persuading	• winning
• problem-solving	• losing
• decision-making	• resolving

Instead, dialogue is about the following:
- seeking understanding
- looking for common ground
- exploring multiple narratives
- surfacing hidden assumptions/judgments/beliefs

When dialogue precedes decision-making, problem-solving, negotiations, or planned execution, it strengthens the quality and improves the outcomes of each of these actions. Taking time to practice dialogue prior to engaging in these activities enhances communication and improves the quality of each action. Hidden assumptions are surfaced, more facts and data are brought into the open, perspectives are broadened, understanding is deepened, and shared understanding is fostered.

I have identified seven practices for dialogue mastery that are helpful for coaches and clients. Each practice has skills that form it. These practices are not linear. They are interdependent. Each practice is inextricably interwoven with the others.

Anyone can use dialogue in a conversation to improve it, even when others in the conversation are not trained in dialogue. Others in the conversation will be influenced by its usage. When dialogue is done well and all members in the conversation are practicing it, each participant consciously commits to engaging in the seven dialogue-mastery practices outlined in the following chart.

Seven Dialogue-Mastery Practices

Practice	Skills
1. **Suspension** • consciously looking at internal thought processes • suspending judgments, assessments, and assumptions • seeing one's personal narrative or the story being told to oneself and willingly setting it aside	self-awareness, introspection
2. **Presence** • consciousness, mindfulness, and intentionality • being present in the moment • avoiding getting stuck in the past or the future • focusing attention on the speaker's present experience (including thoughts, feelings, and sensations) without judgment	active listening, mindfulness
3. **Listening to understand** • suspending your internal voice • stepping outside your personal narrative • actively seeking to understand the other participant's narrative	attentiveness, perspective-taking
4. **Respect** • consciously, genuinely, and compassionately honoring others' right to choose what they believe, say, do, and feel • suspending judgment or attribution	genuineness, compassion
5. **Inquiry** • asking open-ended questions to deepen your understanding of the speaker's personal narrative • perspective-taking • demonstrating curiosity • exploring the speaker's narrative, thoughts, feelings, and behaviors • being with speakers in their experience	empathy, curiosity

6. **Advocacy**	persuasion, self-expression
• expressing your personal narrative • clearly describing what you think and why • making "I" statements to take personal ownership of your narrative • earnestly persuading the listener to believe what you believe • sharing your perspective, vision, and call to action	
7. **Reflection**	insight, contemplation
• internally reflecting on the dialogue process as it unfolds • considering how you are practicing presence, suspension, and listening to understand, respect, inquire, advocate, and reflect	

Now, let's look at the seven dialogue mastery practices in greater depth. Each practice and its supporting skills will be defined, followed by an explanation of how each fits into dialogue mastery. You will see how they are interwoven. Keep in mind that dialogue is not a linear practice. It's dynamic and fluid. Mastery in one dialogue practice influences mastery in the other dialogue practices. When you have mastery in all seven, you have mastery in dialogue.

Practice #1: Suspension

Suspension is the mental act of pausing and consciously looking at one's internal thought processes; suspending judgments; and noticing one's personal narrative or the story told to oneself and intentionally setting it aside. The following are suspension practice skills:

- *self-awareness*—focusing attention on oneself to assess and contrast one's current behavior with one's internal state, standards, values, and preferences

- *introspection*—reflectively looking inward; examining one's own thoughts and feelings; identifying one's personal narrative

When we attempt dialogue without practicing suspension, we lose the opportunity to suspend our own thoughts, assessments, judgments, opinions, and perspectives and be open to focusing on and understanding the other speaker's perspective. If we don't practice suspension in a dialogue, we won't be able to fully practice presence.

Practicing suspension in a dialogue requires us to engage in self-awareness and introspection. Suspension means intentionally and consciously stepping outside oneself; noticing and focusing attention on one's internal thought processes, including judgments, assessments, assumptions, and narratives; and intentionally suspending them. When we can suspend our own personal stories, we position ourselves to be able to hear and understand the speaker's personal story. Suspending our own story helps us avoid defending our own judgments, assessments, and assumptions, and this makes it possible for us to focus on the speaker's perspective.

Practice #2: Presence

Presence involves consciousness, mindfulness, and intentionality; being present in the moment; avoiding getting stuck in the past or the future; and focusing attention on the speaker's present experience (including thoughts, feelings, and sensations) without judgment. The following are presence practice skills:

- *active listening*—listening to and observing the speaker; forming a careful, tentative impression of what the speaker is experiencing; empathically feeding back this impression (verbally and nonverbally)

- *mindfulness*—a technique used to focus one's full attention on the present, experiencing thoughts, feelings, and sensations and not judging them

In *The Seven Habits of Highly Effective People*, Stephen Covey called active listening the "Fifth Habit: Seek first to understand, then to be understood." Most of us did not learn to be present and actively listen in conversations. We were taught instead to talk at one another. We learned to listen for points of view, perspectives, opinions, or preferences different from our own and then formulate a rebuttal that we believed would win the other person over to our way of thinking or believing.

Talking at one another and listening to persuade or advocate for our position limits us in many ways. First, we lose opportunities to explore multiple perspectives. Second, we alienate others and foster defensiveness and division. Third, we jump to conclusions and solutions with limited data. Fourth, we make ill-informed decisions. And finally, we impulsively execute poorly thought-out plans.

Practicing presence in a dialogue combines active listening and mindfulness. Presence means being consciously mindful and intentionally focused in the moment as we listen to and observe the speaker, form an impression of what he or she is experiencing, and empathically reflect back this impression. Presence is about abstaining from projecting our own thoughts and intentions into the past or the future. It's about staying in the present with the person who is talking and attending to what that person is sharing in the conversation.

Practice #3: Listening to Understand

Listening to understand involves suspending your internal voice; stepping outside your personal narrative; and actively seeking to understand the other participant's narratives. The following are practice skills for listening to understand:

- *attentiveness*—defined by the Free Dictionary as "paying close attention; alert or observant. Showing care for the needs or desires of others; caring or courteous"

- *perspective-taking*—the ability to comprehend and take on another person's point of view regarding thoughts, feelings, beliefs, and attitudes

If we fail to listen to understand, we fall out of dialogue and back into talking at one another instead of deeply understanding one another. When we are listening to promote or defend our own narrative, we are unable to listen to and understand the speaker's narrative.

Listening to understand is about suspending your internal voice (suspension) and demonstrating attentiveness while engaging in perspective-taking. It's about paying close attention (presence), showing care for the speaker's perspective, and actively seeking to understand another person's story. This practice demonstrates to the speaker that the listener cares about and willingly seeks to understand what the speaker has to say. It expresses empathy and compassion.

Practice #4: Respect

Respect involves consciously, genuinely, and compassionately honoring others' right to choose what they believe, say, do, and feel, and suspending judgment or attribution. The following are practice skills for respect:

- *genuineness*—being authentic, real, sincere, and without pretense; not counterfeit

- *compassion*—defined by Dictionary.com as "a feeling of deep sympathy and sorrow for another who is stricken by misfortune, accompanied by a strong desire to alleviate the suffering"

When practicing dialogue, respect is critical. Speakers need to know and believe that when they share personal thoughts, perceptions, assumptions, opinions, or experiences, they will be heard without judgment or attribution. When we feel honored and respected, we feel safer about being vulnerable and transparent in a dialogue.

Respect in a dialogue is the process of consciously, genuinely, and compassionately honoring others' right to choose what they believe, say, do, and feel, and suspending judgment or attribution about their narrative. It's about demonstrating curiosity and genuine interest in other people and their stories.

When dialogue participants are practicing suspension, presence, and listening to understand while showing respect for one another, they are creating a safe space for exploration, curiosity, and discovery. When speakers feels respected by listeners, they will feel supported, encouraged, and heard.

Practice #5: Inquiry

Inquiry involves asking open-ended questions to deepen your understanding of the speaker's personal narrative; perspective-taking; demonstrating curiosity; exploring the speaker's narrative, thoughts, feelings, and behaviors; and being with speakers in their experience. The following are inquiry practice skills:

- *empathy*—the act of understanding, being aware of, being sensitive to, and vicariously experiencing the speaker's feelings, thoughts, and experience, either past or present, without having the feelings, thoughts, and experiences fully communicated explicitly by the speaker

- *curiosity*—inquisitive interest in the speaker's narrative, thoughts, feelings, and behaviors, an interest that leads to deeper inquiry

Inquiry in a dialogue occurs when the listener shows an inquisitive interest in the speaker's narrative, thoughts, feelings, and behaviors by asking open-ended questions and empathically supporting the speaker. It's about letting the speaker know the listener is feeling a sense of "me too" with the listener. It's about compassionately (respect) coming alongside the speaker in the present moment (presence) and sharing mutual understanding and awareness (suspension).

When inquiry is practiced alongside suspension, presence, listening to understand, and respect, dialogue flourishes. When speakers believe that listeners genuinely care about them and feel honored and heard without judgment or attribution, they are more willing to vulnerably self-disclose when listeners inquisitively asks open-ended questions.

Practice #6: Advocacy

Advocacy involves expressing your personal narrative; clearly describing what you think and why you think the way you do; making "I" statements to take personal ownership of your narrative; earnestly persuading the listener to believe what you believe; and sharing your perspective, vision, and call to action. The following are advocacy practice skills:

- *persuasion*—the act of moving another party to action by argument or entreaty, or of reasoning earnestly with someone to dissuade from a belief, position, or planned course of action; to plead with; to urge.

- *self-expression*—the act of verbally expressing or nonverbally demonstrating one's individual personality, traits, beliefs, preferences, values, or perspectives

Advocacy is about telling your story with passion and persuasion. It's about moving the

Advocacy works in a dialogue when one speaker at a time is advocating. When one speaker is advocating, the listeners are engaged in suspension, presence, listening to understand, respect, and inquiry. When each dialogue participant has an opportunity to practice advocacy, one speaker at a time, it works to improve the quality of the conversation. When every member in the dialogue has had an opportunity to engage in advocacy, the group can be assured that all perspectives have been shared; all ideas, beliefs, values, and opinions about the topic of discussion have been surfaced; and each member can feel confident about moving into next steps in a meeting or conversation.

When multiple parties to the dialogue engage in the practice of advocacy at the same time, the conversation is no longer a dialogue. It becomes a debate or an argument. The power of advocacy in a dialogue is that each speaker has an opportunity to be heard and to persuade others to believe what they believe, knowing that judgments will be withheld and all points of view will be honored and respected.

Practice #7: Reflection

Reflection involves internally reflecting on the dialogue process as it unfolds and considering how you are practicing presence, suspension, listening to understand, respect, inquiry, advocacy, and reflection. The following are reflection practice skills:

- *insight*—defined by Merriam-Webster as "the power or act of seeing into a situation; the act or result of apprehending the inner nature of things or of seeing intuitively"

- *contemplation*—the act of considering attentively; steadily regarding; deep, reflective thought

Reflection is ongoing throughout the dialogue. It has two applications. First, listeners are reflecting on their dialogue practices. Secondly, listeners are reflecting on the speaker's story and verbal and nonverbal communication.

Reflection is an internal cognitive process in which the listener hears the speaker's verbal and nonverbal communication and attentively reflects on what is being said and what may be left unsaid. It's also about listeners noticing and intuitively considering how their practice of presence, suspension, listening to understand, respect, inquiry, advocacy, and reflection may be supporting and honoring speakers throughout the dialogue.

If reflection is not practiced consistently throughout the dialogue, listeners miss opportunities to notice when they are out of dialogue—and also lose opportunities to reengage in dialogue. When reflection is not practiced, speakers may not feel supported and honored. When all participants in dialogue engage in the seven dialogue mastery practices, dialogue works well. All participants will feel like they had an opportunity to voice their stories. They will feel heard, understood, and supported. Each participant will gain a deeper, broader understanding and awareness of the topics being explored.

When dialogue precedes decision-making or action planning, the decision quality dramatically improves these activities. Dialogue fosters belonging. The following are questions to consider when coaching someone to foster belonging at work, in the community, or on a team:

- What would it look like if you felt a sense of belonging?
- What obstacles or barriers are preventing you from fostering belonging?
- Think of a time when you have successfully fostered belonging (at work, in your community, on your team). What did you do to make it so?
- How could you replicate that experience of fostered belonging in your present circumstances?
- Who could support you in fostering belonging?

Cultivating Courage

> The foundation of courage is vulnerability—the ability to navigate uncertainty,
> risk, and emotional exposure. It takes courage to open ourselves up to joy.
> —Brené Brown, *Braving the Wilderness*

The skill of cultivating courage involves intentionally choosing to face and embrace our emotions—the things we cannot control—and respond with purposeful action to dispel fear and nurture love. It's developing the mental and moral strength to venture into or withstand dangers or difficulties. We master the skill by developing our mental and moral strength to withstand dangers or difficulties. It's about intentionally choosing to face and embrace our difficult emotional reactions by increasing our emotional intelligence, learning to impulsively react less frequently, and intentionally responding more often to dangers and difficulties.

As we coach clients around creating authentic engagement, cultivating courage often arises for the client as an important coaching agenda item. It's important to partner with clients in exploring how they can cultivate and practice being courageous. Courage is the mental or moral strength to venture into, persevere through, or withstand danger or difficulty. According to Mark Twain, in his novel Pudd'nhead Wilson, "Courage is resistance to fear, mastery of fear—not absence of fear." It's the ability to face fear and dispel it.

The word *courage* comes from the Latin root word *cor*, which means "heart." Courage in its earliest forms meant speaking one's mind by telling all of one's heart. It meant facing our emotions and taking purposeful action to dispel fear and nurture love.

Cultivating courage helps create opportunities for authentic engagement. When we feel safe, we are more willing to engage in responsibly risking and being vulnerable with one another. When courage is cultivated, trust is extended, strengthened, and rebuilt (actionable trust), and authentic engagement becomes possible. The following are questions to consider when coaching someone to cultivate courage at work, in the community, or on a team:

- What would it look like if you felt courageous?
- What would be different for you if you were able to cultivate more courage?
- What obstacles or barriers are preventing you from being courageous?
- What is a first step you could take toward cultivating courage?
- Think of a time when you have successfully cultivated courage. What did you do to make it so?
- How could you replicate that experience of cultivated courage in your present circumstances?
- Who could support you in cultivating courage?
- What resources do you need to help you cultivate courage?
- What role models do you have who have successfully cultivated courage?

AUTHENTIC ENGAGEMENT DERAILERS

Three enduring themes in derailment research by Ellen Van Velsor and Jean Brittain Leslie (1995) apply to authentic engagement:

1. **Problems with interpersonal relationships**
   When leaders have problems with interpersonal relationships, employees become disengaged. This creates isolation and poorly performing teams. When subordinates are disengaged, it's much more challenging to manage and mold them.

2. **Inability to change or adapt during a transition**
   Leaders who lack the ability to change or adapt during a transition risk becoming disengaged and fearful. They may struggle with feeling misaligned with critical mission areas and functions. Often, they become preoccupied with wanting to return to the way things were instead of embracing change.

3. **Inability to build and lead a team**
   When leaders fail to build and lead high-performing teams, their subordinates suffer from isolation, disengagement, mistrust, and fear.

OPM's Fundamental Competencies cluster has one competency, interpersonal skills, that has one derailer that applies to practice two:

- **Treats others with courtesy and respect**
  Leaders who fail to treat others with courtesy and respect risk derailment because subordinates will be preoccupied with fear: fear of retaliation, retribution, marginalization, exclusion, and loss of connection. Employees who feel they have been treated discourteously or disrespectfully will isolate and withdraw. Instead of focusing on their jobs, they will become preoccupied with their rights, complaints, and perceived mistreatment.

ECQ: Leading People has three competencies with derailers that apply:

1. **Conflict Management**
   - **Manages and resolves conflicts effectively**
     Leaders who struggle with effectively managing and resolving conflict frequently have to work harder at conflict management. Conflict avoidance is the most frequent strategy employed by leaders who struggle with this competency. When conflict is avoided, it escalates over time. The effort required to resolve it dramatically increases with this escalation. Coaching leaders to develop mastery in conflict management and to step into conflict sooner will help them avoid this derailer.

2. **Leveraging Diversity**
   - **Respects cultural, religious, gender, and racial differences**
   When leaders fail to demonstrate respect toward coworkers around cultural, religious, gender, and racial differences, they risk derailment. Coaching leaders to understand and appreciate differences and to learn about their own unconscious bias, stereotypes, and personal differences can help avoid this derailer.

3. **Team Building**
   - **Inspires pride and team spirit among team members**
   Leaders who fail to inspire pride and team spirit among team members risk derailment because their teams will likely underperform and may fail to meet critical mission requirements. Coaching leaders to dispel fear, foster belonging, and cultivate courage will help them avoid this derailer.

   - **Builds teams of appropriate size and structure to accomplish work goals**
   When teams are not structured or sized properly, work goals are at risk. Coaching leaders to know their people, foster and nurture belonging, and cultivate the courage to speak out when things are misaligned will help to avoid this derailer.

When you are coaching a leader who may be at risk for derailment around these themes and competencies, you may want to partner with the client to explore developing mastery in authentic engagement. By working with the client to strengthen competency in the three authentic engagement skills—dispelling fear, fostering belonging, and cultivating courage—you can assist them in managing these potential derailers.

Use the themes and behaviors checklist to identify potential derailment themes and behaviors you would like to work on in coaching. Check off those that have been a challenge or source of tension, or those that may benefit from further reflection and exploration.

Practice Two: Authentic Engagement	Derailment Themes*	Derailment Behaviors*
❐ Dispel fear ❐ Foster belonging ❐ Cultivate courage	❐ Problems with interpersonal relationships	❐ Insensitive to others ❐ Cold, aloof ❐ Arrogant ❐ Overly ambitious ❐ Authoritarian ❐ Poor relationships ❐ Organizational isolation ❐ Poor working relations ❐ Does not treat others with courtesy and respect ❐ Does not manage and resolve conflicts effectively ❐ Does not respect cultural, religious, gender, and racial differences ❐ Does not lead without micromanaging
	❐ Inability to change or adapt during a transition	❐ Conflict with upper management ❐ Fails to adapt to organizational change ❐ Is not open to new ideas and opinions from others
	❐ Inability to build and lead a team	❐ Inability to build a team ❐ Inability to lead a team ❐ Does not inspire pride and team spirit among team members ❐ Does not build teams of appropriate size and structure to accomplish work goals

*Derailment Themes adapted from *Themes in Derailment Research* (Van Velsor and Leslie 1995, Table 1). Derailment Behaviors adapted from *Themes in Derailment Research* (Van Velsor and Leslie 1995), OPM Leadership 360.

CHAPTER SUMMARY

Authentic engagement is the practice of genuinely and authentically connecting with others. It's about dispelling fear and loving one another. It's about creating and fostering a sense of belonging—the belief that we are a part of something bigger than ourselves. And it's about cultivating the courage to be vulnerable and open to joy, compassion, meaning, and purpose. The following are authentic engagement skills:

- **Dispelling fear**—the act of reacting unconsciously and impulsively less frequently and responding consciously and intentionally more frequently to strong emotions. Dispelling fear is the act of shifting one's emotional and physiological states from fear and stress to love and relaxation.

- **Fostering belonging**—the act of being who you are, deeply believing in yourself, and courageously sharing your authentic self with others. Fostering belonging means discovering sacredness in both taking a stand when facing the unknown alone and becoming a part of something bigger than yourself in connection with others who share a belief in something meaningful and purposeful.

- **Cultivating courage**—the act of intentionally choosing to face and embrace emotions (the things you cannot control) and responding with purposeful action to dispel fear and nurture love. Cultivating courage involves developing the mental and moral strength to venture into or withstand dangers or difficulties.

Crosswalk: OPM ECQs and Competencies and Practice Two: Authentic Engagement

OPM ECQs and Competencies*	Practice Two: Authentic Engagement
Fundamental Competencies	
Interpersonal Skills: Treats others with courtesy, sensitivity, and respect. Considers and responds appropriately to the needs and feelings of different people in different situations.	• dispelling fear • fostering belonging • cultivating courage
Oral Communication: Makes clear and convincing oral presentations. Listens effectively; clarifies information as needed.	• fostering belonging

ECQ: Leading People This core qualification involves the ability to lead people toward meeting the organization's vision, mission, and goals. Inherent to this ECQ is the ability to provide an inclusive workplace that fosters the development of others, facilitates cooperation and teamwork, and supports constructive resolution of conflicts.	
Leveraging Diversity: Fosters an inclusive workplace where diversity and individual differences are valued and leveraged to achieve the vision and mission of the organization.	• dispelling fear • fostering belonging • cultivating courage
Team Building: Inspires and fosters team commitment, spirit, pride, and trust. Facilitates cooperation and motivates team members to accomplish group goals.	• dispelling fear • fostering belonging
ECQ: Building Coalitions This core qualification involves the ability to build coalitions internally and with other Federal agencies, State and local governments, nonprofit and private sector organizations, foreign governments, or international organizations to achieve common goals.	
Partnering: Develops networks and builds alliances; collaborates across boundaries to build strategic relationships and achieve common goals.	• dispelling fear • fostering belonging • cultivating courage
Political Savvy: Identifies internal and external politics that impact the work of the organization. Perceives organizational and political reality and acts accordingly.	• fostering belonging
Influencing/Negotiating: Persuades others; builds consensus through give and take; gains cooperation from others to obtain information and accomplish goals.	• dispelling fear • fostering belonging • cultivating courage

*OPM ECQs and Competencies quoted from OPM Executive Core Qualifications, https://www.opm.gov/policy-data-oversight/senior-executive-service/executive-core-qualifications/.

RESOURCES

Books, Articles, Videos

Bishop, Scott R., Mark Lau, Shauna L. Shapiro, Linda Carlson, Nicole D. Anderson, James Carmody, Gerald Devins. 2004. "Mindfulness: A Proposed Operational Definition." *Clinical Psychology: Science and Practice*, 11: 230–241.

Block, Peter. 1987. *The Empowered Manager: Positive Political Skills at Work*. San Francisco: Jossey-Bass.

Bossidy, Larry, and Ram Charan. 2002. *Execution: The Discipline of Getting Things Done*. New York: Crown Business.

Bradberry, Travis, and Jean Greaves. 2009. *Emotional Intelligence 2.0*. San Diego, CA: TalentSmart.

Brown, Brené. 2017a. *Braving the Wilderness. The Quest for True Belonging and the Courage to Stand Alone*. New York: Random House.

———. 2017b. *Rising Strong. How the Ability to Reset Transforms the Way We Live, Love, Parent, and Lead*. New York: Random House.

Buckingham, Marcus, and Donald O. Clifton. 2001. *Now, Discover Your Strengths*. New York: Free Press.

———. 2007. *Go Put Your Strengths to Work. 6 Powerful Steps to Achieve Outstanding Performance*. New York: Free Press.

Burgess, Tobin, Kevin Pugh, and Leo Sevigny. 2007. *The Personal Vision Workbook*. Clifton Park, *NY*: Thomson Delmar Learning.

Chapman, Gary, and Paul White. 2019. *The Five Languages of Appreciation in the Workplace*. Chicago: Northfield Publishing Empowering Organizations by Encouraging People.

Cherniss, Carey, and Daniel Goleman. 2001. *The Emotionally Intelligent Workplace*. San Francisco: Jossey-Bass.

Covey, Stephen R. 2004. *The Seven Habits of Highly Effective People. Powerful Lessons in Personal Change*. New York: Simon and Shuster.

Crum, Thomas. 2006. *Three Deep Breaths. Finding Power and Purpose in a Stressed-Out World*. San Francisco: Barrett Koehler Publications, Inc.

DeBecker, Gavin. 1999. *The Gift of Fear: This Book Can Save Your Life and Other Survival Signals That Protect Us from Violence*. New York: Dell Publishing.

Deluca, Joel R. 1999. *Political Savvy: Systematic Approaches to Leadership Behind-the-Scenes*. Pittsburgh: EBG Publications.

"Dictionary.com." Dictionary.com. Accessed July 22, 2019. https://www.dictionary.com/.

"Dictionary by Merriam-Webster: America's Most-trusted Online Dictionary." Merriam-Webster. Accessed July 22, 2019. https://www.merriam-webster.com/.

"Dictionary, Encyclopedia and Thesaurus." The Free Dictionary. Accessed July 22, 2019. https://www.thefreedictionary.com/.

Eblin, Scott. 2011. *The Next Level: What Insiders Know about Executive Success*, 2nd ed. Boston: Nicholas Brealey Publishing.

Friedman, Edwin H. 2007. *Failure of Nerve: Leadership in the Age of the Quick Fix.* New York: Church Publishing, Inc.

Goleman, Daniel. 1998. *Working with Emotional Intelligence.* New York: Bantam.

Goleman, Daniel, Richard Boyatzis, and Annie McKee. 2002. *Primal Leadership: Realizing the Power of Emotional Intelligence.* Boston: Harvard Business School Press.

Harter, Jim. 2018. *Employee Engagement on the Rise in the U.S.* Gallup News, August 26. Retrieved from http://news.gallup.com/poll/241649/employee-engagement-rise.aspx.

Heath, Chip, and Dan Heath. 2017. *The Power of Moments.* New York: Simon and Schuster.

Hoppe, Michael H. 2006. *Active Listening: Improve Your Ability to Listen and Lead.* Greensboro: CCL Press Publications.

Isaacs, William. 1999. *Dialogue and the Art of Thinking Together.* New York: Doubleday.

Jabr, Ferris. 2012. "Does Self-Awareness Require a Complex Brain?" *Scientific American,* August 22. Retrieved from https://blogs.scientificamerican.com/brainwaves/does-self-awareness-require-a-complex-brain/.

Knight, Mary. 2013. "Three Strategies for Making Employee Engagement Stick." *Gallup Business Journal.* Retrieved from http://businessjournal.gallup.com/content/159851/three-strategies-making-employee-engagement-stick.aspx.

Kouzes, James M., and Barry Posner. 2017. *The Leadership Challenge,* 6th ed. Hoboken, NJ: John Wiley and Sons, Inc.

Kznaric, Roman. 2013. "The Ancient Greeks' 6 Words for Love (And Why Knowing Them Can Change Your Life)." *Yes!* March 9. Retrieved from https://www.yesmagazine.org/happiness/the-ancient-greeks-6-words-for-love-and-why-knowing-them-can-change-your-life.

Lee, Guss, and Diane Elliott-Lee. 2006. *Courage: The Backbone of Leadership.* San Francisco: Jossey-Bass.

Loehr, Jim. 2007. *The Power of Story: Change Your Story, Change Your Destiny in Business and in Life.* New York: Free Press.

Markman, Art. 2015. "Is Perspective-Taking a Skill?" *Psychology Today,* October 22. Retrieved from https://www.psychologytoday.com/us/blog/ulterior-motives/201510/is-perspective-taking-skill.

Stein, Steven J., and Howard E. Book. 2011. *The EQ Edge: Emotional Intelligence and Your Success.* 3rd ed. San Francisco: Jossey-Bass.

Suzuki, Shunryu. 2011. *Zen Mind, Beginner's Mind: Informal Talks on Zen Meditation and Practice.* Boston: Shambala Publications, Inc.

Van Velsor, Ellen, and Jean Brittain Leslie. 1995. "Why Executives Derail: Perspectives Across Time and Cultures." *Academy of Management Executive* 9 (4): 62–72.

Walker, Karen Thompson. 2013. "What Fear Can Teach Us." TED 2013. https://www.youtube.com/watch?time_continue=85&v=OwgWkUIm9Gc.

Wheatley, Margaret. 2009. *Turning to One Another: Simple Conversations to Restore Hope to the Future*, 2nd ed. San Francisco: Barrett Koehler Publications, Inc.

Wiseman, Theresa. 1996. "A Concept Analysis of Empathy." *Journal of Advanced Nursing*, 23: 1162–1167.

Recommended Assessments

EQ-i 2.0 Model of Emotional Intelligence Leadership Report® (Multi Health Systems)
Four leadership dimensions: authenticity, coaching, insight, and innovation.
Five dimensions and fifteen subscales of EQ:
1. Self-perception (self-regard, self-actualization, emotional self-awareness)
2. Self-expression (emotional expression, assertiveness, independence)
3. Interpersonal (interpersonal relationships, empathy, social responsibility)
4. Decision-making (problem solving, reality testing, impulse control)
5. Stress management (flexibility, stress tolerance, optimism)

Everything DiSC Work of Leaders Profile® (Inscape Publishing)
Measures how you approach the most fundamental work of leaders:
- **creating a vision**—exploration, boldness, testing assumptions
- **alignment**—clarity, dialogue, inspiration
- **execution**—momentum, structure, feedback

Influence Style Indicator® (Discovery Learning/Multihealth Systems)
Measures five influence preferences: asserting, inspiring, bridging, negotiating, and rationalizing.

Leadership Practices Inventory® (LPI) (Jossey-Bass/Pfeiffer)
Measures five leadership practices and thirty leadership behaviors, six per practice:
1. **Model the way.**
   - I set a personal example of what I expect of others.
   - I spend time and energy making certain that the people I work with adhere to the principles and standards I have agreed on.
   - I follow through on the promises and commitments that I make.
   - I ask for feedback on how my actions affect other people's performance.
   - I build consensus around a common set of values for running our organization.
   - I am clear about my philosophy of leadership.

2. **Inspire a shared vision.**
   - I talk about future trends that will influence how our work gets done.
   - I describe a compelling image of what our future could be like.
   - I appeal to others to share an exciting dream of the future.
   - I show others how their long-term interests can be realized by enlisting in a common vision.
   - I paint the "big picture" of what I aspire to accomplish.
   - I speak with genuine conviction about the higher meaning and purpose of our work.

3. **Challenge the process.**
   - I seek out challenging opportunities that test my own skills and abilities.
   - I challenge people to try out new and innovative ways to do their work.
   - I search outside the formal boundaries of my organization for innovative ways to improve what I do.
   - I ask "What can I learn?" when things don't go as expected.
   - I make certain that I set achievable goals, make concrete plans, and establish measurable milestones for the projects and programs that I work on.
   - I experiment and take risks, even when there is a chance of failure.

4. **Enable others to act.**
   - I develop cooperative relationships among the people I work with.
   - I actively listen to diverse points of view.
   - I treat others with dignity and respect.
   - I support the decisions that people make on their own.
   - I give people a great deal of freedom and choice in deciding how to do their work.
   - I ensure that people grow in their jobs by learning new skills and developing themselves.

5. **Encourage the heart.**
   - I praise people for a job well done.
   - I make it a point to let people know about my confidence in their abilities.
   - I make sure that people are creatively rewarded for their contributions to the success of our projects.
   - I publicly recognize people who exemplify commitment to shared values.
   - I find ways to celebrate accomplishments.
   - I give the members of the team lots of appreciation and support for their contributions.

OPM Leadership 360 (US Office of Personnel Management)
Measures the fundamental competencies and the five executive core qualifications (ECQs), including the twenty-two supporting leadership competencies.

PRACTICE THREE:
Aligned Accountability

Empathy alone will never promote the self-organization necessary for learning from experience ... the emphasis here, however, is ... on conformity of behavior to the democratic process. It is in this sense that promoting in others the initiative to be accountable is far more critical to the health of an institution than trying to be understanding or insightful.

—Edwin H. Friedman, *A Failure of Nerve*

Michael returned for coaching about four weeks later.

Coach: Michael, welcome back. It's good to see you again.

Client: Thanks, John. It's good to see you again too.

Coach: How would you like to use our time together today?

Client: I'd like to talk about my conversation with my tech lead and some events that happened the following two weeks. First, I met with him the next day after our last conversation. I thought it went well. He understood the impact his behavior had on our team from missing the important project deadline, and he outlined a plan to be consistent at meeting future deadlines. I thought everything was resolved. Little did I know about what was coming!

The following week, another key project milestone came due, and he missed that deadline by forty-eight hours. He also failed to submit his quarterly project reports on time. I did talk with him about both instances right when they occurred, but I didn't put any kind of corrective action plan in place.

My last experience with human resources, legal, and my supervisor was disappointing. When I tried to do the right thing with an employee who wasn't performing, they didn't support me, and my supervisor directed me to drop the corrective action plan and forget about any consequences.

In light of that experience, I'm not confident about trying that approach again. Now I'm concerned that my tech lead's behavior pattern is going to continue, and I'm worried about how the rest of my team is going feel about me not holding him accountable.

Coach: What would you need to have happen to bolster your confidence to do the right thing in this instance?

Client: My biggest struggle is my lack of confidence in my leadership and my fear of not getting their support. I remember my supervisor telling me that if I had consulted with him sooner in the process, he could have helped me with my documentation and with understanding policy requirements for disciplinary action. Accepting that it was partially my fault because I hadn't followed policy and documented sufficiently is something I've been avoiding. Sitting down with my supervisor and asking for support and guidance is probably my best approach before I do anything else.

Coach: When will you take that next step?

Client: I'll talk with my supervisor this afternoon.

Coach: What else do you need to bolster your confidence?

Client: As we talk about it, I'm realizing that it's really a lack of self-confidence on my part rather than a lack of confidence in my leadership. I need the courage to ask for help and to take the high road and do the right thing even though it's going to be hard.

Coach: How can you strengthen your courage?

Client: I believe that if I just do it, meet with my supervisor, and follow through with corrective discipline, I'll gain courage and confidence. I know that's logically my next step, and I'm willing to commit to taking those actions by starting my conversation with my supervisor this afternoon.

Coach: Is there anything else around this topic that would be helpful for you to explore in the time we have left, or do you have another direction you'd like to go today?

Client: I think I need to work on a couple more things. One is clarifying standards with everyone on my team, and another is rewarding people consistently when they effectively execute mission priority tasks.

Coach: Which of those two is a higher priority for you?

Client: Clarifying standards would be first. Until these are clear, I know I'll continue to have difficulties rewarding people for the right things.

Coach: Where could you begin to tackle clarifying standards for your team?

Client: First, I think I need more clarity about our agency's strategic priorities. I know a plan gets published every year, but I'm not really familiar with it. Getting it out and reading it would be a good start. Then I could talk with my supervisor about how our division priorities align with the agency's strategy. Once I know those things, I could look for ways to tie my employees' performance objectives to our division priorities.

Coach: When do you think you could accomplish those tasks?

Client: It'll take me a few weeks to do all those things. I'll get started on it early next week though.

Coach: What would your next step be after that?

Client: Then I could clearly identify my employees' mission contributions, tie them back to their performance plans, and reward them consistently.

Coach: It sounds like you have several action steps to take over the next several weeks. Is there anything else you want to talk about before we end our time together today?

Client: No. I feel like I have some solid action steps to take and a clear direction forward.

Coach: Great. Would you be willing to summarize your action plan for moving forward?

Client: Sure. First, I'm going to meet with my supervisor this afternoon and ask for help. Next, I am going to work on getting clarity on standards by reading the agency's strategic plan. Then, in two weeks, I'll talk with my supervisor about how our division priorities align with the agency's strategy. Once I know those things, I will look for ways to tie my employees' performance objectives to our division priorities. After I've accomplished these tasks, I can clearly identify my employees' mission contributions, tie them back to their performance plans, and reward them consistently.

Michael's Action Steps

1. Meet with my supervisor this afternoon and ask for help.
2. Work on getting clarity on agency standards by reading the strategic plan, then talking with my supervisor about how our division priorities align with agency strategies.
3. Look for opportunities to tie my employees' performance objectives to our division priorities and clearly identify opportunities to consistently reward their mission contributions.

MASTERING ALIGNED ACCOUNTABILITY

> Accountability is the glue that ties commitment to the result.
> —Bob Proctor

Aligned accountability is the practice of clarifying standards for yourself and others; holding everyone, including yourself, accountable to the standards; and providing direct feedback. We master aligned accountability by learning and consistently taking advantage of every opportunity to practice these three skills.

Coaches foster accountability with their clients by partnering with them to set goals, design and commit to actions, and inquire about their clients' goal progress in each coaching session. Coaches also set the example by following through with commitments to their clients like showing up on time for appointments, managing the time for coaching sessions, promptly sending out any promised resources, and returning calls and emails from clients. When your coaching clients want to cultivate accountability as part of their coaching agenda, it's important to help them explore and define their desired actions around clarifying standards for themselves and others, holding themselves and others accountable to those standards, and identifying ways to provide direct feedback to others on accountability expectations.

Self-responsibility, or personal responsibility, is a critical precursor to accountability. Avoiding personal responsibility seems to be the path of least resistance for many people. They conclude that it's easier to blame people, places, and things for their personal circumstances than it is to stop and ask, "What's my part in this?" If we are unwilling to own the consequences of our choices and actions, we will be unable to hold ourselves accountable. When we are unable or unwilling to hold ourselves accountable, it becomes extremely difficult to hold others accountable.

When we coach leaders to assume self-responsibility, we empower them to maximize their effectiveness at engaging and leading others. By taking personal responsibility for words and deeds, leaders set the example for others to follow in their footsteps. When leaders are self-responsible, they see more options and choices that they may be blinded to when avoiding personal responsibility.

By practicing self-responsibility, we make it possible to hold ourselves and others accountable. When we take ownership (accountability) of our actions, we set the example for others to do the same. Accepting consequences for our own actions models the way for others when we clarify standards and hold them accountable for their actions too.

CLARIFYING STANDARDS

> Exemplary leaders' goals and standards are unambiguous,
> helping people focus on what needs to be done.
> —James Kouzes and Barry Pozner, *The Leadership Challenge*

The skill of clarifying standards involves spelling out specific criteria or action steps that one expects of oneself or another for the successful execution of goals, tasks, or activities. Coaches can help their clients master the skill by ensuring that they make performance expectations clear. This includes defining how performance will be measured, evaluated, and rewarded. We partner with them to ensure that they and others understand the standards and that they have clarity about how they and others are expected to perform.

Clarifying standards helps clients with aligning accountability by assisting them in spelling out the specific criteria or action steps they expect of themselves or from others for activities like performance, goals, and deliverables. When people understand the standards and are clear about how they are expected to perform, they will be able to confidently align their actions with the standards to which they will hold themselves or others accountable.

When we are working on clarifying standards with others, remember that it's something that occurs within the context of a relationship. We need to know our people—their strengths, challenges, passions, interests, skills, and growth areas. We need to know what fuels their passion and gives them meaning and purpose. Building on these insights, we can tailor our communication with them to bring more clarity to standards and a deeper understanding about how they can connect what they do to mission priorities.

In a coaching conversation, it's critical to have the client clarify standards for desired outcomes. Clients set the agenda and identify what they wish to achieve in the coaching session. The coach partners with the client to cocreate the agenda and clarify standards for measuring the client's successful execution of those goals. Some clients may be seeking coaching on how to improve accountability with direct reports. In these instances, it's important to coach the client around clarifying standards with those direct reports.

When coaching someone to clarify standards, consider the following questions as they relate to the client and the client's employee(s), team, and organization:
- How will clarifying standards be of benefit?
- Think of a time when standards were clear. What was the impact?
- What standards are already clear?
- What makes them clear?
- What standards have you identified that need clarity?
- What's missing that would bring clarity?
- Who could assist you in clarifying these standards?
- How will you know when you have clarity around standards?

Consider the following questions when coaching a client to help someone else clarify standards:
- How can you determine your direct report's clarity around standards?
- What could you encourage that person to do to help them clarify standards?
- What have you tried in the past with others that led to success in clarifying standards?
- Who could assist you in helping others to clarify standards?
- How will you know when your direct report has clarity around standards?

HOLDING EVERYONE ACCOUNTABLE

Leaders strengthen others when they make it possible to exercise choice and discretion, when they design options and alternatives to the ways that work and services are produced, and when they foster accountability and responsibility that compel action.
—James Kouzes and Barry Pozner, *The Leadership Challenge*

The skill of holding everyone accountable involves clarifying expectations, offers, promises, and responsibilities among all parties. Its purpose is to create consistency and compel action toward mission execution. We start to master the skill by assessing those expectations, responsibilities, offers, and promises. Next, all stakeholders participate in a dialogue to create shared understanding around all areas in which accountability is expected by exploring diverse perspectives/viewpoints, surfacing hidden assumptions, and deepening awareness and understanding of complex ideas, challenges, and options.

Holding everyone accountable creates consistency and compels action. When coaching a client, it's critical that you as a coach hold clients accountable by engaging them in a conversation about how they will hold themselves accountable or seek out an accountability partner. Occasionally, the coach may agree to serve as an accountability partner to the client. On these occasions, the coach and client partner together to cocreate clear standards and actions that both parties will follow.

When clients commit to holding themselves accountable, the coach partners with them to cocreate an action plan that includes standards, action steps, and criteria for measuring success. Sometimes a client may choose to ask a colleague or friend to serve as an accountability partner. In these instances, the coach partners with the client to clarify how to make a request for an accountability partnership. This request needs to include expectations that both parties will have of one another.

When coaching someone to hold everyone accountable, consider the following questions regarding your client and your client's employee(s), team, and organization:

- What is your piece in this situation?
- What are the costs of not holding everyone accountable?
- What are the benefits of holding everyone accountable?
- What would it mean?
- What barriers or obstacles are preventing you from holding everyone accountable?
- Who could support you in holding everyone accountable?
- What resources do you need to hold everyone accountable?
- What strategies have served you well in the past for holding everyone accountable?
- How have you seen others effectively hold everyone accountable?

PROVIDING DIRECT FEEDBACK

> We all need people who will give us feedback. That's how we improve.
> —Bill Gates

The skill of providing direct feedback involves directly and clearly providing feedback to another person that clarifies the context in which an event occurred, words that were spoken and actions that were observed, the observer's interpretation of the observed words and actions, and the observer's request for future actions. We master the skill of providing direct feedback by learning and practicing the FAIR feedback method.

Sometimes it's necessary for the coach to provide direct feedback to clients when the topic of accountability is being explored as part of the client's agenda and action planning. The coach may ask for permission to share an observation with the client about the client's accountability actions. If the client is receptive, the coach can share observations and engage the client in deeper conversation around accountability.

On other occasions, the client may have a goal to provide feedback to a direct report. The coach can partner with the client to cocreate a feedback message. When providing direct feedback, it's helpful to use the FAIR feedback method to format your message. The method is outlined in the chart that follows.

Consider the following questions when coaching someone to provide direct feedback:

- Who has given you helpful feedback and what was helpful about how they delivered it?
- Whose feedback-receiving skills do you admire, and what can you learn from them?
- What barriers are holding you back from providing direct feedback when it's needed?
- What would help you take the first step in providing direct feedback?
- How could you prepare for your next opportunity to provide direct feedback?

We master aligned accountability by first fostering actionable trust—extending, strengthening, and rebuilding trust as necessary in all our relationships. With trust present, we nurture authentic engagement by dispelling fear, fostering belonging, and cultivating courage. This positions us to master aligned accountability by clarifying standards, holding everyone accountable to those standards, and providing direct feedback that clarifies standards and reinforces expectations.

FAIR Feedback Method

Step	Actions
Frame	Frame the context. Describe when the actions occurred. Specify as many facts as you can about the context, such as the date, day, time,
Actions	Describe the actions you observed. What did you hear the person say? What did you observe the person doing? Identify the words you heard and/or the actions you observed. Consider including a description of the speaker's voice rate, pitch, and volume if appropriate. You may also include observations of gestures, posture, and facial expressions. Avoid sharing your assessments, judgments, and opinions.
Interpretation	Explain your interpretation of the actions you observed and described. Use "I" statements to take ownership of your story. Identify and share what you believe happened to you as a result of the actions you saw and heard.

	Make a request, if appropriate, identifying what you would appreciate from the person in the future. Make "I" statements. Describe behaviors and languages you would prefer as an alternative to what you experienced.
Request	

The following are examples of the FAIR feedback method:

Coach feedback to client

Coach: In our last coaching session (*Frame*), you said, "It's important to me to begin taking steps to improve my resilience. I will start doing aerobic exercises and weight training four days a week. I will begin following a healthy eating plan. I want to lose two pounds weekly over the next six weeks. I will begin on Monday." Today, in our coaching session, you told me that you went to the gym two days out of seven last week, you followed your healthy eating plan four out of seven days, and you lost one pound. You said, "I am discouraged with my progress. I want to get back on track" (*Actions*). It appears to me that you have fallen short of your goals. I'm hearing you say it's important to you to get on track. What barriers or obstacles are keeping you from success? How can you remove or mitigate these barriers or obstacles? What support do you need (*Requests*)?

Client feedback to direct report

Client: Frank, last Monday in our weekly 10:00 a.m. meeting (*Frame*) you told me, "I will submit the completed project budget to you by the close of business on Friday this week." Today is Monday, and I haven't received your completed project budget (*Actions*). I'm feeling disappointed by your failure to keep your commitment. I'm now late with my project progress report to my supervisor because I don't have your completed project budget to include in it (*Interpretation*). When can you have the completed project budget ready for me? What steps can you take to avoid missing important project deadlines in the future (*Request*)?

ALIGNED ACCOUNTABILITY DERAILERS

Two enduring themes in derailment research by Ellen Van Velsor and Jean Brittain Leslie (1995) apply to aligned accountability:

1. **Failure to meet business objectives**
   When leaders fail to manage or hold subordinates accountable for poor performance, they are at risk for failing to meet business objectives.

2. **Inability to build and lead a team**

   When leaders fail to clarify standards, hold everyone accountable, and provide direct feedback they are at risk for failing to build and lead a team.

OPM's ECQ: Results Driven has one competency with a derailer that applies to practice three;

1. **Competency: Accountability**
   - **Achieves results within set time frames**

     Leaders who fail to achieve results within set time frames frequently need to develop competence in clarifying standards, holding everyone on the team accountable, and consistently providing direct feedback.

When you are coaching a leader who fails to meet business objectives, has an inability to build and lead a team, or fails to achieve results within set time frames, it may be helpful to partner with the client to achieve mastery of aligned accountability by developing competence in the three supporting skills: clarifying standards, holding everyone accountable, and providing direct feedback.

Use this checklist to identify potential derailment themes and behaviors you would like to work on in coaching. Check off those that have been a challenge or a source of tension, or those that may benefit from further reflection and exploration.

Practice Three: Aligned Accountability	Derailment Themes*	Derailment Behaviors*
❏ Clarify standards ❏ Hold everyone accountable ❏ Provide direct feedback	❏ Failure to meet business objectives	❏ Poor performance ❏ Fails to achieve results within set time frames ❏ Lack of follow-through ❏ Lack of hard work ❏ Overly ambitious
	❏ Inability to build and lead a team	❏ Inability to build a team ❏ Inability to lead a team ❏ Failing to staff effectively ❏ Can't manage subordinates

*Derailment Themes adapted from *Themes in Derailment Research* (Van Velsor and Leslie 1995, Table 1). Derailment Behaviors adapted from *Themes in Derailment Research* (Van Velsor and Leslie 1995), OPM Leadership 360.

CHAPTER SUMMARY

Aligned accountability is the practice of clarifying standards for yourself and others; holding everyone, including yourself, accountable to the standards; and providing direct feedback. The following are aligned accountability skills:

- **Clarifying standards**—the act of spelling out specific criteria or action steps that one expects of oneself or of another for the successful execution of goals, tasks, or activities.

- **Holding everyone accountable**—the act of consistently holding everyone involved accountable. It's about clarifying expectations, commitments, and responsibilities among all parties. Its purpose is to create consistency and compel action toward mission execution.

- **Provide direct feedback**—the act of directly and clearly providing feedback to another person that clarifies the context in which an event occurred; words that were spoken and actions that were observed; the observer's interpretation of the observed words and actions; and the observer's request for future actions.

Crosswalk: OPM ECQs and Competencies and Practice Three: Aligned Accountability

OPM ECQs and Competencies	Practice Three: Aligned Accountability
Fundamental Competencies	
Oral Communication: Makes clear and convincing oral presentations. Listens effectively; clarifies information as needed.	• providing direct feedback
ECQ: Leading People This core qualification involves the ability to lead people toward meeting the organization's vision, mission, and goals. Inherent to this ECQ is the ability to provide an inclusive workplace that fosters the development of others, facilitates cooperation and teamwork, and supports constructive resolution of conflicts.	
Developing Others: Develops the ability of others to perform and contribute to the organization by providing ongoing feedback and by providing opportunities to learn through formal and informal methods.	• providing direct feedback

ECQ: Results Driven	
This core qualification involves the ability to meet organizational goals and customer expectations. Inherent to this ECQ is the ability to make decisions that produce high-quality results by applying technical knowledge, analyzing problems, and calculating risks.	
Accountability: Holds self and others accountable for measurable high-quality, timely, and cost-effective results. Determines objectives, sets priorities, and delegates work. Accepts responsibility for mistakes. Complies with established control systems and rules.	clarify standards, hold everyone accountable, provide direct feedback
ECQ: Business Acumen	
This core qualification involves the ability to manage human, financial, and information resources strategically.	
Human Capital Management: Builds and manages workforce based on organizational goals, budget considerations, and staffing needs. Ensures that employees are appropriately recruited, selected, appraised, and rewarded; takes action to address performance problems. Manages a multisector workforce and a variety of work situations.	clarify standards, hold everyone accountable

RESOURCES

Books, Articles, Videos

Bregman, Peter. 2016. "The Right Way to Hold People Accountable." *Harvard Business Review*, January 11.

Chapman, Gary, and Paul White. 2019. *The Five Languages of Appreciation in the Workplace.* Chicago: Northfield Publishing Empowering Organizations by Encouraging People.

Cottrell, David. 2002. *Monday Morning Leadership: 8 Mentoring Sessions You Can't Afford to Miss.* Dallas: Cornerstone Leadership Institute.

Dweck, Carol S. 2016. *Mindset: The New Psychology of Success: How We Can Learn to Fulfill Our Potential.* New York: Ballantine Books.

Friedman, Edwin H. 2007. *A Failure of Nerve: Leadership in the Age of the Quick Fix.* New York: Church Publishing, Inc.

Kouzes, James M., and Barry Posner. 2017. *The Leadership Challenge*, 6th ed. Hoboken, NJ: John Wiley and Sons, Inc.

Leonard, George. 1992. *Mastery: The Keys to Success and Long-Term Fulfillment.* New York: Penguin Group, Random House.

Van Velsor, Ellen, and Jean Brittain Leslie. 1995. "Why Executives Derail: Perspectives across Time and Cultures." *Academy of Management Executive* 9 (4): 62–72.

Recommended Assessments

Benchmarks 360® (Center for Creative Leadership)

Sixteen skills: resourcefulness; doing whatever it takes; being a quick study; decisiveness; leading employees; confronting problem employees; participative management; change management; building and mending relationships; compassion and sensitivity; straightforwardness and composure; balance between personal life and work; self-awareness; putting people at ease; differences matter; career management

Coaching Behaviors Inventory® (Noer Consulting)
Measures three coaching behavior areas (www.davidnoer.com):
1. *Assessing:* data-gathering, gap analysis, goal-setting, measurement/feedback
2. *Challenging:* confronting, focusing/shaping, reframing, empowering/energizing
3. *Supporting:* attending, inquiring, reflecting, affirming

Everything DiSC 363™ for Leaders® (Inscape Publishing)
Eight approaches and twenty-four practices to effective leadership:
1. Pioneering (promoting bold action, stretching the boundaries, finding opportunities)
2. Energizing (showing enthusiasm, building professional networks, rallying people to achieve goals)
3. Affirming (being approachable, acknowledging contributions, creating a positive environment)
4. Inclusive (staying open to input, showing diplomacy, facilitating dialogue)
5. Humble (being fair-minded, showing modesty, maintaining composure)
6. Deliberate (providing a sense of stability, promoting disciplined analysis, communicating with clarity)
7. Resolute (improving methods, speaking up about problems, setting high expectations)
8. Commanding (focusing on results, taking charge, showing confidence)

Everything DiSC Work of Leaders Profile® (Inscape Publishing)
Measures how you approach the most fundamental work of leaders:
- **creating a vision**—exploration, boldness, testing assumptions
- **alignment**—clarity, dialogue, inspiration
- **execution**—momentum, structure, feedback

Five Behaviors of a Cohesive Team® (Inscape Publishing)
A team assessment that measures a team's five behaviors that contribute to building cohesive teams: trust one another, engage in conflict around ideas, commit to decisions, hold one another accountable, and focus on achieving collective results.

Leadership Practices Inventory® (LPI) (Jossey-Bass/Pfeiffer)
Measures five leadership practices and thirty leadership behaviors, six per practice:

1. **Model the way.**
   - I set a personal example of what I expect of others.
   - I spend time and energy making certain that the people I work with adhere to the principles and standards I have agreed on.
   - I follow through on the promises and commitments that I make.
   - I ask for feedback on how my actions affect other people's performance.
   - I build consensus around a common set of values for running our organization.
   - I am clear about my philosophy of leadership.
2. **Inspire a shared vision.**
   - I talk about future trends that will influence how our work gets done.
   - I describe a compelling image of what our future could be like.
   - I appeal to others to share an exciting dream of the future.
   - I show others how their long-term interests can be realized by enlisting in a common vision.
   - I paint the "big picture" of what I aspire to accomplish.
   - I speak with genuine conviction about the higher meaning and purpose of our work.
3. **Challenge the process.**
   - I seek out challenging opportunities that test my own skills and abilities.
   - I challenge people to try out new and innovative ways to do their work.
   - I search outside the formal boundaries of my organization for innovative ways to improve what I do.
   - I ask "What can I learn?" when things don't go as expected.
   - I make certain that I set achievable goals, make concrete plans, and establish measurable milestones for the projects and programs that I work on.
   - I experiment and take risks, even when there is a chance of failure.
4. **Enable others to act.**
   - I develop cooperative relationships among the people I work with.
   - I actively listen to diverse points of view.
   - I treat others with dignity and respect.
   - I support the decisions that people make on their own.
   - I give people a great deal of freedom and choice in deciding how to do their work.
   - I ensure that people grow in their jobs by learning new skills and developing themselves.

5. **Encourage the heart.**
    - I praise people for a job well done.
    - I make it a point to let people know about my confidence in their abilities.
    - I make sure that people are creatively rewarded for their contributions to the success of our projects.
    - I publicly recognize people who exemplify commitment to shared values.
    - I find ways to celebrate accomplishments.
    - I give the members of the team lots of appreciation and support for their contributions.

OPM Leadership 360 (US Office of Personnel Management)
Measures the fundamental competencies and the five executive core qualifications (ECQs), including the twenty-two supporting leadership competencies.

Styles and Climates Survey® (Korn Ferry)
This assessment consists of two 180-degree online assessment tools. Together, they give you a picture of the leadership style you use and a revealing view of the impact this has on your team. The six leadership styles assessed are: directive, visionary, affiliative, participative, pacesetting, and coaching. The six organizational climates assessed are: clarity, rewards, standards, responsibility, flexibility, and team commitment.

viaEDGE® (Korn Ferry)
A self-assessment to provide insight into learning agility and assist in determining potential. It provides scores on five dimensions—mental agility, people agility, change agility, results agility, and self-awareness—and on overall learning agility.

CHAPTER 4

PRACTICE FOUR:

Adaptive Learning and Mastery

What is mastery? It resists definition yet can be instantly recognized. It comes in many varieties, yet follows certain unchanging laws. It brings rich rewards, yet is not really a goal or a destination but rather a process, a journey. We call this journey mastery.

—George Leonard, *Mastery*

Five weeks later, Michael returned for his next coaching conversation.

Client: These past several weeks have really flown by quickly. I'm excited to share my progress with you since our last conversation!

Coach: I'm delighted to hear that you've been so productive since our last meeting. Where would you like to begin?

Client: First, I'd like to give you a progress update. In our last meeting, I committed to getting more clarity about our agency's strategic priorities. I got a copy of the strategic plan and read it. I took some notes and met with my supervisor to get more clarity about how our division priorities align with the agency's strategy. That was a very helpful conversation.

Then, in my next couple of staff meetings, I shared highlights of the agency's strategic plan and our division's priorities. This was a struggle at first. Several team members complained that there were too many strategies and that it's impossible to do all of them well. We talked about this, and another point that surfaced was the perspective that the strategies didn't seem to connect to our mission. Others felt that our customers were frustrated, too, because they were hearing that we were going to stop doing some of the things that they really valued and needed.

I realized that I couldn't clearly connect all the strategies to our mission either. I told the team that I'd meet again with my leadership and get more information to help us all make these connections.

After talking with my manager again, I was able to help my team make the connections between the various strategies and our mission. We took time in the next staff meeting to discuss this new information. In the end, it was a fruitful discussion that brought clarity and focus to the team.

Now I'm reviewing each of my performance objectives, and I'm making notes for individual conversations with each of them to talk about how we can more closely align performance objectives with the agency's strategy and our division's priorities. Once I have these pieces in place, I can begin rewarding people's mission contributions and acknowledging the clear ties back to our strategy.

Coach: You've made significant progress in a short time frame. Congratulations! Is there anything else you want to explore about these actions that might be helpful to your ongoing progress?

Client: No. I think I'm on track. I do want to talk about another topic though. I want to explore curiosity. I've learned in some of my leadership classes that it's important to embrace curiosity. I know that this would help me be open to new, innovative, and creative approaches, and I struggle with wanting to hold on to how I've always done things. The tried and true gives me comfort, and it's been effective. The other practice I've been taught is to adopt a beginner's mind when I am trying new things. This sounds so easy, but it's really quite difficult!

Coach: As you think about curiosity and a beginner's mind, what would be most helpful to you to explore first?

Client: I think I'd like to explore both together. I remember George Leonard said in his book *Mastery* (1992), "And for all who walk the path of mastery, however far that journey has progressed, Kano's request becomes a lingering question, an ever-new challenge: Are you willing to wear your white belt?"

When I think about that quote and my struggle with trying new approaches, I realize that my pride is getting in the way. I have confidence in the way I've always done things, and I get scared when I am asked to try new approaches because I don't have past performance and successes to fall back on to bolster my confidence. I'm afraid of failing or not getting it right, and because of those fears, I frequently don't try new things or practice curiosity to explore possibilities.

Coach: What would it mean to you to wear your white belt when faced with new possibilities or new ways of doing your work?

Client: If I could make that shift, I believe two changes would occur. First, I'd probably not avoid trying out new things as often as I do now. And secondly, I probably wouldn't rely on what I know is an excuse to avoid being open and curious about what I don't know and exploring new possibilities.

Coach: What barriers are keeping you from wearing your white belt right now?

Client: It's that fear again! I'm afraid of failing or looking foolish. Now that I see that, I think my path forward is practicing my breathing when I find myself feeling that fear of failing or looking foolish. It worked well for me with my fear of conflict and my fear of not being good enough, so I can't see why it wouldn't serve me well with these fears too.

Coach: Would you be willing to try an exercise now?

Client: Sure.

Coach: I invite you to imagine that you are at work. You've just left a meeting with your supervisor, and he's asked you to take the lead on a new pilot project. The technology is new, and you won't have much time to get up to speed before implementing it with your team. Take a moment now to notice what you're feeling. What emotions are present, and where do you feel them in your body?

Client: I'm feeling some anxiety and some insecurity. I don't want to disappoint my supervisor, and I want to lead the new pilot project effectively. My palms are clammy, my breathing is getting shallow, I have some tightness in my neck and shoulders, and I can't seem to concentrate on much else right now.

Coach: What steps can you take right now to shift your emotions from anxiety and insecurity to calmness and confidence?

Client: I can change my breathing. I'm going to do that now.

Michael took three slow, full, deep breaths. With each inhalation, he held the breath to a count of ten. Then he exhaled, holding the exhalation to a count of ten.

Coach: Now, what do you notice about your emotions and your body?

Client: I'm feeling calmer and more relaxed. My palms are drying, my breathing is regular, and the tightness in my neck and shoulders is nearly gone too. My concentration is back, and I can actually focus on possibilities instead of survival from failure.

Coach: How can you apply this learning in the future?

Client: I need to remember that my breathing influences my emotions in every circumstance. I've been practicing two to three times a day as a relaxation technique; now I see that I can use it whenever I'm noticing myself experiencing physical signs of stress or emotions that follow those somatic signals.

Coach: What would help you remember to breathe?

Client: I'll add it to my journaling. I've been tracking my relaxation exercises. Now I can also track opportunities where I'm feeling stressed. This will help me look for patterns. Then I can pay attention in the future and connect the patterns to my breathing.

Coach: What do you anticipate being different in the future for you as you incorporate these new strategies?

Client: I expect that I'll feel calmer and more confident when I'm facing new opportunities or new ways of working. As I get more consistent with managing my breathing, I think I can also expect to have less anxiousness and fear as well.

Coach: We're coming to the end of our time together today. Is there anything else you'd like to explore before we wrap up our conversation?

Client: No. I'm feeling confident and prepared now to take the next steps in my leadership development journey. I'm committing to practicing my breathing beyond the two or three times a day I've been doing it for relaxation to help me manage my anxiousness and fear of not being good enough.

Additionally, I'm going to use my journaling to track my opportunities to use my breathing to build my self-confidence and identify patterns where I need to use my breathing effectively. This will help me increase my somatic awareness and improve my self-regulation.

Finally, I'm going to finish my review of my employees' performance objectives and schedule conversations with them to talk about how we can more closely align performance objectives with the agency's strategy and our division's priorities. This will prepare me to be able to award my people for their mission contributions and effective efforts.

Coach: That sounds like a solid plan. I think your passion for growing as a leader is remarkable, and I applaud your commitment and focused efforts to stretch yourself outside your comfort zone and try out new ways of leading. It's my honor and privilege to be your coach. We've reached the end of our time together for today. Let's look at our calendars and schedule our next conversation.

Michael's Action Steps

1. Practice breathing to help manage my anxiety and fear of not being good enough.

2. Track opportunities and patterns in my journal where I can effectively use my breathing to build my self-confidence.

3. Finish my review of my employees' performance objectives, and schedule conversations to discuss aligning their performance with agency strategies and division priorities.

4. Consistently award effective employee contributions to mission.

MASTERING ADAPTIVE LEARNING

Adaptive learning and mastery is the practice of embracing curiosity and acknowledging that we don't know what we don't know. It's about adopting a beginner's mind; embracing curiosity and new possibilities; and embracing the concept of failing faster to learn and grow and improve more quickly. We master adaptive learning by acquiring these skills and taking advantage of every opportunity we encounter to use them.

When a coaching client chooses to focus the coaching agenda on adaptive learning and mastery, the coach partners with the client to explore the necessary skills. The client is encouraged to fully explore embracing curiosity. This skill is about shifting your mindset from performing to practicing. It's about exploring possibilities and opportunities for learning. It's about looking for more than one right answer to problems and challenges.

EMBRACING CURIOSITY

> When we are curious, we view tough situations more creatively
> and have less defensive reactions to stress.
> —Francesca Gino, "The Business Case for Curiosity"

The skill of embracing curiosity involves acknowledging that we don't know what we don't know. It's about embracing challenges and asking, "What if?" We master this skill by acknowledging that we don't know what we don't know. We intentionally explore more possibilities, and we look for possibilities that may have been unseen. We learn to look at situations that used to trigger fear and stress as new opportunities for growth and learning.

When coaches and clients embrace curiosity, they expand their opportunities for learning. They explore more possibilities. Defensive reactions to fear and stress diminish. Tough situations begin to appear more manageable. Previously unseen answers emerge. They embrace looking for more than the first right answer or the one right solution.

Embracing curiosity is the starting point on the journey toward continuous adaptive learning and mastery. We encourage our clients to take the first step by acknowledging that they don't know what they don't know. We challenge them to be open to new possibilities, different options, and alternative perspectives.

In their book *Introducing Neuro-linguistic Programming* (1993), Joseph O'Connor and John Seymour called this *unconscious incompetence*, the first stage of the four stages of learning. The second stage is *conscious incompetence*—we know that we don't know. Stage three is *conscious competence*: when we focus and concentrate without distraction, we can perform the learned skill. *Unconscious competence* is the fourth stage—the stage of skill mastery. We have muscle memory, and we can perform the skill without conscious effort.

Four Learning Stages
Stage one: unconscious incompetence
Stage two: conscious incompetence
Stage three: conscious competence
Stage four: unconscious competence

If you had never played tennis and you decided to begin learning how to play, you would be in the first learning stage, unconscious incompetence. You wouldn't know what you didn't know about the skills and strategies of playing tennis.

After a few tennis lessons, you would move into stage two, conscious incompetence. Now you would know what you didn't know about the skills and strategies of playing tennis. Your coach would be putting you through various skill drills and giving you homework practice assignments. You would understand that the objective is to hit the ball over the net and have it land inside the marked court boundaries; however, you would not be able to consistently accomplish this each time you hit the tennis ball.

With continuing lessons, you would understand the mechanics of the various strokes in tennis like serves, lobs, forehand, backhand, and net volleys. At this third stage, you would be moving into conscious competence. With concentrated effort and minimal distractions, you would be able to execute the various tennis strokes with competence. The fourth stage, unconscious competence, occurs when you reach mastery of tennis. At this stage, you have muscle memory. You can execute the right stroke at the right time with accuracy and strategy. You don't have to think about it; it seems to come naturally.

When our coaching clients want to explore the skill of embracing curiosity, we partner with them to begin to look at situations that used to trigger fear and stress as new opportunities for growth and learning. We challenge them to embrace challenges, asking, "What if?" Consider the following questions when coaching someone to embrace curiosity:

- Ask yourself, "What if?"
- What would happen if you refrained from settling for the first possible solution?
- What would happen if you thought more in depth about this situation, opportunity, event, or challenge?
- What would embracing curiosity look like for you?
- How could you look for more than one right answer?
- What else could you consider in these circumstances?
- How would challenging the status quo serve you, your employee, your team, and your organization in this situation?
- How could you view this situation as an opportunity to grow and learn?

ADOPTING A BEGINNER'S MIND

In the beginner's mind there are many possibilities, in the expert's mind there are few.
—Shunryu Suzuki, *Zen Mind, Beginner's Mind*

The skill of adopting a beginner's mind involves approaching learning with openness, curiosity, and a vision of new possibilities. It's about accepting not knowing and being willing to experiment and practice new behaviors to deepen and broaden learning. We master the skill by letting go of seeing ourselves as the expert. We approach learning with an open, curious mind. We envision new possibilities and opportunities.

Coaches and clients both benefit from mastering this skill. For coaches, it's often about letting go of being the expert, of wanting to fix it for a client or provide a solution, and of knowing what's best for the client. When we are coaching clients who want to explore adopting a beginner's mind, we partner with them to explore opportunities for doing so. This builds on embracing curiosity and prepares them for the third skill: failing faster.

When we adopt a beginner's mind, we build on the earlier mind-set of embracing curiosity. Beginners approach learning with openness, curiosity, and a vision of new possibilities. They can acknowledge that they don't know what they don't know—the first stage of learning. Remember Michael's quote from *Mastery* by George Leonard? "And for all who walk the path of mastery, however far that journey has progressed, Kano's request becomes a lingering question, an ever-new challenge: Are you willing to wear your white belt?"

Sometimes a struggle arises within us when we are faced with the option of adopting a beginner's mind. On the one hand, we want to be recognized for what we already know or what we are already capable of doing. On the other hand, we know, too, that before we can fully embrace new learning opportunities, we must be willing to consciously and intentionally set aside what we know and what we know we can do. This mind-set shift positions us to willingly embrace curiosity on the path toward practicing adaptive learning and mastery.

Consider the following questions when coaching someone to adopt a beginner's mind:

- Imagine you have not yet learned everything you know about your current situation. What would your fresh new perspective be?
- If you had a blank slate to work with, what would you create?
- Imagine there were no constraints, barriers, or obstacles present. What choices would you make? What actions would you take?
- If this was your first time approaching this situation, what would you do first?
- What barriers are holding you back from adopting a beginner's mind?
- How could you change your self-talk to empower yourself to adopt a beginner's mind in this situation?

FAILING FASTER

> Make it "good enough," ship it, improve it based on market feedback,
> rinse and repeat. This approach attains a solution much faster
> because of the snowball effect of iterative learning.
> —Sunnie Giles, "How to Fail Faster—and Why You Should"

The skill of failing faster involves shifting one's mind-set from seeing failure as a reflection of one's personal incompetence to a perspective of viewing failure as an opportunity for new learning. It's approaching failure as an opportunity for gleaning feedback for improvement and new learning. We master the skill by reflecting on our failures and looking for lessons learned. We intentionally let go of perceiving failure as a reflection of our personal incompetence. We embrace failure as a feedback mechanism for new learning. We let go of our fear of failure and embrace curiosity and openness.

When our coaching clients choose to explore developing the skill of failing faster, we partner with them to reflect on their personal stories about failing. We provide direct communication and our interpretations of what we hear, and we challenge them to consider reframing failing as a learning opportunity.

> You fail all the time, but you aren't a failure until you start blaming someone else.
> —Bum Phillips

When we see failure as a reflection of our personal incompetence or lack of self-worth, we often react with feelings of fear. Fear in these instances can take many forms, including failure, unworthiness, incompetence, exclusion (removed from a team, customer account, project, or position), and judgment. When we reframe failing as a learning opportunity, it's easier for us to embrace the mind-set of being willing to fail faster. Seeing product or service failures as valuable feedback for improvement creates opportunities for new learning.

This shift in mind-set to accepting failure as a learning opportunity often comes more naturally to those with a behavioral style of dominance, as determined by an Everything DiSC® assessment or a temperament type of thinking as determined by the MBTI Step II® assessment. These styles and types tend to separate who they are as people from the task at hand. They have strong preferences for being task-oriented or data-oriented. They tend not to personalize the results of their efforts.

Alternatively, people with a behavioral style of conscientiousness, as determined by an Everything DiSC® assessment, can tend to personalize failure. These individuals are also task-oriented like the dominance style; however, they have tendencies toward perfectionism, value "doing it right," and can be very sensitive to criticism. Individuals with a feeling preference on the MBTI also tend to share this perspective on failure.

Any behavioral style or temperament type can learn to flex into a mind-set of failing faster. When this mind-set is contrary to one's natural preferences, it takes conscious, intentional effort, and it expends more energy. When coaching someone to fail faster, consider the following questions:

- What do you need to feel safe at failing faster?
- What would happen if you substituted a good-enough solution for a fail-safe solution?
- How could you shift toward embracing failure as a step toward radical innovation?
- How could you create an environment for your employee(s), team, branch, office, or organization to freely experiment and serendipitously generate new ideas and strategies?
- How might you present your employees with moderate challenges or stretch opportunities that they could struggle through and resolve?
- What could you do to promote iterative learning on your team?

- If flexing into a failing-faster mind-set expends energy for you, what might you do to manage your capacity for resiliency?

To attain adaptive learning and mastery, start with mastery of the first three practices. Foster actionable trust by extending, strengthening, and rebuilding trust in all your relationships. Build on this by nurturing authentic engagement, which is accomplished by dispelling fear, fostering belonging, and cultivating courage among everyone in the organization. Then create a culture of aligned accountability by clarifying standards, holding everyone accountable to those standards, and providing direct feedback on performance to the standards. Finally, embrace curiosity, adopt a beginner's mind, and learn to fail faster.

ADAPTIVE LEARNING AND MASTERY DERAILERS

Two enduring themes in derailment research by Ellen Van Velsor and Jean Brittain Leslie (1995) apply to adaptive learning and mastery:

- **Inability to change or adapt during a transition**
  When leaders are unable to develop or adapt to new situations, they are at risk for being unable to change or adapt during a transition.

- **Failure to meet business objectives**
  When leaders perform poorly, they are at risk for failure to meet business objectives.

Of OPM's Fundamental Competencies, one, continual learning, and the OPM category: organizational impact, both have one derailer that applies to practice four:

1. **Continual Learning**
   - **Learns from mistakes**
     Leaders who fail to chain results to their actions; reflect on mistakes and failures; and identify lessons learned are at risk of repeating these same mistakes and failures. Coaching clients to pursue continual learning by conducting post mortems or after-action reviews assists them in improving their continual learning

2. **Organizational Impact**
   (This category of questions appears in the OPM Leadership 360 assessment. Questions about these behaviors are not asked of the person taking the assessment, the person's raters are asked to answer them about the person being assessed).

   - **Recognizes personal strengths and weaknesses**
     Underlying all the derailment themes is the concept of self-awareness. Leaders who are unable to recognize their strengths and weaknesses are at a significant disadvantage when it comes to maximizing impact on the agency's mission and strategic initiatives.

Use this checklist to identify potential derailment themes and behaviors you would like to work on in coaching. Check off those that may have been a challenge or a source of tension, or those that may benefit from further reflection and exploration.

Practice Four: Adaptive Learning and Mastery	Derailment Themes*	Derailment Behaviors*
❑ Embrace curiosity ❑ Adopt a beginner's mind ❑ Fail faster	❑ Inability to change or adapt during a transition ❑ Failure to meet business objectives	❑ Unable to develop or adapt ❑ Does not recognize his or her strengths and weaknesses ❑ Too narrow business experience ❑ Narrow functional orientation ❑ Not prepared for promotion ❑ Poor performance

* Derailment Research adapted from *Themes in Derailment Research* (Van Velsor and Leslie 1995, Table 1). Derailment Behaviors adapted from *Themes in Derailment Research* (Van Velsor and Leslie 1995), OPM Leadership 360.

CHAPTER SUMMARY

Adaptive learning and mastery is the practice of acknowledging that we don't know what we don't know; adopting a beginner's mind; embracing curiosity and new possibilities; and adopting the concept of failing faster to learn and grow and improve more quickly. The following are adapted learning and mastery skills:

- **Embracing curiosity**—the act of acknowledging that we don't know what we don't know. It's about embracing challenges and asking, "What if?"

- **Adopting a beginner's mind**—the act of approaching learning with openness, curiosity, and a vision of new possibilities. It's about accepting not knowing and being willing to experiment and practice new behaviors to deepen and broaden learning.

- **Failing faster**—the act of shifting one's mind-set from seeing failure as a reflection of personal incompetence to viewing it as an opportunity for learning. It's approaching failure as an opportunity for gaining feedback for improvement.

Crosswalk: OPM ECQs and Competencies and Practice Four: Adaptive Learning and Mastery

OPM ECQs and Competencies	Practice Four: Adaptive Learning and Mastery
Fundamental Competencies	
Continual Learning: Assesses and recognizes own strengths and weaknesses; pursues self-development.	• embracing curiosity • adopting a beginner's mind • failing faster
ECQ: Leading Change This core qualification involves the ability to bring about strategic change, both within and outside the organization, to meet organizational goals. Inherent to this ECQ is the ability to establish an organizational vision and to implement it in a continuously changing environment.	
Creativity and Innovation: Develops new insights into situations; questions conventional approaches; encourages new ideas and innovations; designs and implements new or cutting-edge programs/processes.	• embracing curiosity • adopting a beginner's mind • failing faster

*OPM ECQs and Competencies quoted from OPM Executive Core Qualifications, https://www.opm.gov/policy-data-oversight/senior-executive-service/executive-core-qualifications/.

RESOURCES

Books, Articles, Videos

Bishop, Scott R., Mark Lau, Shauna Shapiro, Linda Carlson, Nicole D. Anderson, James Carmody, Zindel V. Segal, Susan Abbey, Michael Speca, Drew Velting, and Gerald Devins. 2004. "Mindfulness: A Proposed Operational Definition." *Clinical Psychology: Science and Practice*, 11: 230–241.

Boser, Ulrich. 2018. "Learning Is a Learned Behavior. Here's How to Get Better at It." *Harvard Business Review*, May 2.

Buckingham, Marcus, and Donald O. Clifton. 2001. *Now, Discover Your Strengths*. New York: Free Press.

———. 2007. *Go Put Your Strengths to Work: 6 Powerful Steps to Achieve Outstanding Performance*. New York: Free Press.

Cottrell, David. 2002. *Monday Morning Leadership: 8 Mentoring Sessions You Can't Afford to Miss.* Dallas: Cornerstone Leadership Institute.

Dethmer, Jim, Diana Chapman, and Kaley Warner Klemp. 2014. *The 15 Commitments of Conscious Leadership.* KaleyKlemp.com.

Dweck, Carol S. 2016. *Mindset: The New Psychology of Success: How We Can Learn to Fulfill Our Potential.* New York: Ballantine Books.

Edmondson, Amy C. 2004. "Psychological Safety, Trust, and Learning in Organizations: A Group-Level Lens. In *Trust and Distrust in Organizations*, edited by Roderick Kramer and Karen Cook. New York: Russell Sage Foundation.

Friedman, Edwin H. 2007. *Failure of Nerve: Leadership in the Age of the Quick Fix.* New York: Church Publishing, Inc.

Giles, Sunnie. 2018. "How to Fail Faster—and Why You Should." *Forbes*, April 30. Retrieved on February 17, 2018 from: https://www.forbes.com/sites/sunniegiles/2018/04/30/how-to-fail-faster-and-why-you-should/#44d85d1cc177.

Gino, Francesca, Todd B. Kashdan, David J. Disabato, and Fallon R. Goodman. 2018. "The Business Case for Curiosity." *Harvard Business Review*, September–October: 14.

Gladwell, Malcolm. 2008. *Outliers: The Story of Success.* New York: Little, Brown.

Goldsmith, Marshall, and Mark Reiter. 2007. *What Got You Here Won't Get You There.* New York: Hyperion.

Harris, Russ. 2013. *Getting Unstuck in ACT: A Clinician's Guide to Overcoming Common Obstacles in Acceptance and Commitment Therapy.* Oakland, CA: New Harbinger Publications, Inc.

Heath, Chip, and Dan Heath. 2017. *The Power of Moments.* New York: Simon and Schuster.

Kahneman, Daniel. 2011. *Thinking Fast and Slow.* New York: Farrar, Straus, and Giroux.

Leonard, George. 1992. *Mastery: The Keys to Success and Long-Term Fulfillment.* New York: Penguin Group, Random House.

Mikkelsen, Kenneth, and Harold Jarched. 2015. "The Best Leaders Are Constant Learners." *Harvard Business Review*, October 16.

O'Connor, Joseph, and John Seymour. 1993. *Introducing Neuro-Linguistic Programming: Psychological Skills for Understanding and Influencing People*, rev. ed. Hammersmith, London: Aquarian Press.

Pink, Daniel. 2018. *When: The Scientific Secrets of Perfect Timing.* New York: Penguin Random House LLC.

Suzuki, Shunryu. 2011. *Zen Mind, Beginner's Mind: Informal Talks on Zen Meditation and Practice.* Boston: Shambala Publications, Inc.

Van Velsor, Ellen, and Jean Brittain Leslie. 1995. "Why Executives Derail: Perspectives across Time and Cultures." *Academy of Management Executive* 9 (4): 62–72.

Recommended Assessments

Everything DiSC Management Profile® (Inscape Publishing)
Everything DiSC Management Profile focuses on your DiSC management style, directing and delegating, motivating, developing others, and working with your manager. Participants learn about their strengths and challenges as managers and how to adapt to meet the needs of the people they manage, making them more effective managers.

Everything DiSC Workplace Profile® (Inscape Publishing)
Measures how you approach the most fundamental work of leaders:
- **creating a vision**—exploration, boldness, testing assumptions
- **alignment**—clarity, dialogue, inspiration
- **execution**—momentum, structure, feedback

MBTI Step II® (The Myers Briggs Company)
The Step II report is an in-depth personalized description of your personality preferences derived from your answers to the Myers-Briggs Type Indicator® instrument. It includes your four-letter type along with some of the unique ways that you express your type. The MBTI® instrument was developed by Isabel Myers and Katharine Briggs as an application of Carl Jung's theory of psychological types. This theory suggests that we have opposite ways of gaining energy (extraversion or introversion), gathering or becoming aware of information (sensing or intuition), deciding or coming to a conclusion about that information (thinking or feeling), and dealing with the world around us (judging or perceiving).

OPM Leadership 360 (United States Office of Personnel Management)
Measures the fundamental competencies and the five executive core qualifications (ECQs), including the twenty-two supporting leadership competencies.

viaEDGE® (Korn Ferry)
A self-assessment to provide insight into learning agility and assist in determining potential. It provides scores on five dimensions: mental agility, people agility, change agility, results agility, and self-awareness—and on overall learning agility.

CHAPTER 5

PRACTICE FIVE:

Aptly Navigating Complexity, Chaos, and Ambiguity

Successful leaders must be able to adjust on the fly while acquiring knowledge and skills that can be accessed in similar situations in the future. They must be cognitively nimble and quick to ascertain the essence of a challenge, and they must rapidly reach potential conclusions. They have a passion for turning even the most trying of circumstances into learning opportunities.

—Tim Flanagan and John Lybarger, *Leading Forward*

Michael began our next coaching conversation with a check-in:

Client: Since our last meeting, I've made progress on several fronts. I've been journaling regularly about my experiences of anxiousness and a fear of not being good enough. By using my breathing exercises, I've been able to frequently shift my emotions and somatic responses to calmness and a sense of confidence in being good enough. I've also finished my review of my employees' performance objectives, and I have one-on-one conversations scheduled to talk about how we can more closely align their individual performance objectives with the agency's strategy and our division's priorities.

Coach: You've made significant progress. How are you feeling about the work you've completed?

Client: I feel optimistic and confident. Now that I have a plan to move forward, I'm feeling good about the future.

Coach: What is important to you to talk about during our time together today?

Client: The main obstacles I'm facing right now are navigating through the complexity, chaos, ambiguity, and constant change I face day in and day out. When I get overwhelmed by the complexity, I lose confidence in my decision-making. Amid chaos, I struggle with uncertainty and lack of direction.

Growing up in the agency, I was constantly recognized and rewarded for my technical competence. I didn't struggle with ambiguity when I was engineering software, or designing a new system, or managing complex projects. Now, as a leader, I'm expected to make strategic decisions and cascade change effort visions when the way forward is ambiguous and the future is uncertain.

Coach: What do you believe you need to address right now?

Client: I think the most important thing for me right now is my struggle with uncertainty and lack of direction when I'm in the midst of chaos.

Coach: What is important for you to have when you're in the midst of chaos?

Client: I need to learn to be comfortable with not knowing. The chaos and uncertainty aren't going to diminish anytime soon. If anything, they'll probably become more frequent!

Coach: When you have more comfort with not knowing, what will be different for you?

Client: I'll have more confidence, and I'll be able to live with the lack of direction.

Coach: What do you believe you need to achieve more comfort with not knowing?

Client: I've done some reading, and I've learned that I need to increase my adaptability, flexibility, and resilience. The first step for me is to practice hitting the pause button. When I get impatient and feel like I have to get something done quickly, I need to stop, breathe, think it through, and then intentionally carry out a plan.

Coach: What barriers are keeping you from taking these steps?

Client: I know what to do. I just have to remember to do it!

Coach: What would help you with remembering?

Client: It goes back to my breathing once again, doesn't it! I can add this to my journaling. When I find myself confronting uncertainty and chaos, I can journal about it, track practicing my breathing, and look for shifts in my ability to more consistently pause and think. This will probably reduce my impulse to react quickly, and it will increase my intentional, thoughtful responses.

Coach: Is there anything else about confronting uncertainty and chaos that is important for you to explore now?

Client: No. I'm feeling confident about my plan to work on it. I think the next thing I want to explore is strengthening my resiliency. Work is taxing and draining when I'm prioritizing multiple mission taskings and several change initiatives all at the same time.

Coach: What do you believe you need to do to strengthen your resiliency?

Client: I remember from my leadership courses at the agency that resiliency is about bouncing back, making a quick recovery, and springing back to life and to work. For some people, it comes naturally; for others, it has to be learned. I think the latter is more my situation!

I read in your book *Leading Forward* that it's also learned from lessons of experience. The second thing I remember is that tenacity and enthusiasm play important roles in building resiliency too. Tenacity is about being persistent, with great resolve. It's about steadfast determination to get the job done despite obstacles and barriers. Enthusiasm is contagious. When leaders display genuine and spirited enthusiasm in the face of difficulties, those around them find a reason to engage.

Coach: As you think about what you've learned and read regarding resiliency, what would be most meaningful for you in the moment?

Client: I'm not at a loss for opportunities to learn from experience! They seem to be all around me. I guess my challenge is figuring out how to take advantage of these lessons of experience instead of letting them slip by without learning from them.

Coach: As you think about taking advantage of these opportunities, what feelings are you aware of?

Client: It's anxiety and fear again! I mean, what if I miss important lessons? What if I keep doing the same things I've always done and fail to change and grow?

Coach: What have you learned about your anxiety and fear that might serve you in these circumstances?

Client: At the risk of sounding like a soundtrack set to loop, it goes back to my breathing and journaling once again. I know in my head that breath is important. I just keep missing the connections in new circumstances!

Coach: How will you apply what you know in this instance?

Client: I'm going to continue looking for patterns and capture them in my journal. I will practice breathing whenever I feel like my resilience is being tapped or depleted, and I will watch for opportunities to be optimistic and enthusiastic instead of anxious and fearful. I'm confident that my deep breathing will continue to shift my emotions and my mood.

Coach: We're coming to the end of our time together today. What have you learned in today's conversation, and how will you take it forward?

Client: I've learned four things. First, I can gain confidence and comfort with not knowing by practicing my breathing exercises and building my resiliency. Second, I can increase my resiliency by learning from my experiences. This includes pausing and reflecting, impulsively reacting less, and intentionally responding more to challenging situations. Third, I've been reminded that I can strengthen my tenacity by being more persistent and having more resolve. And fourth, I can practice my breathing to shift my emotions from anxiety and fear to enthusiasm and optimism.

Coach: You continue to make steady progress. I applaud your enthusiasm and effort to stretch and grow yourself as a leader. Let's look at our calendars and schedule your next session.

Michael's Action Steps

1. I will build my confidence and comfort with chaos and ambiguity by practicing my breathing.
2. I will increase my resiliency capacity by learning from my experiences, pausing and reflecting, impulsively reacting less, and intentionally responding more in challenging situations.
3. I will strengthen my tenacity by being more persistent and having more resolve throughout the day.
4. I will practice my breathing when I am feeling anxiety and fear to shift my emotions to enthusiasm and optimism.

MASTERING COMPLEXITY, CHAOS, AND AMBIGUITY

Aptly navigating complexity, chaos, and ambiguity is the practice of accepting that you don't know all the answers, questions, data, circumstances, barriers, obstacles, or opportunities. It's about building resiliency so that you can bounce back from hardships and challenging circumstances. It means learning to respond intentionally more frequently and to react impulsively less often in the face of complexity, chaos, and ambiguity. We master the ability to navigate complexity, chaos, and ambiguity by learning three skills: shifting our mind-set to accept not knowing; investing effort in behaviors that build resilience; and intentionally choosing to respond more and react less in the midst of complexity, chaos, and ambiguity.

Coaches and clients both benefit from mastering this fifth practice. Our world is becoming increasingly more complex, chaotic, and ambiguous every day. In the midst of big data, advancing technological breakthroughs, increased data storage capacity, faster data access, and ever more demanding customers wanting instant answers, solutions, responses, and products, we can become paralyzed and immobilized. If we attempt to hold on to the traditional ways of managing information and delivering products and solutions with 95-percent-plus confidence, we set ourselves up for fear and obsolescence. Shifting our mind-set from striving for the perfect solution or product to striving for agility, flexibility, adaptability, and resilience will help us master the skill of aptly navigating complexity, chaos, and ambiguity. It's really about stepping outside our comfort zones; letting ourselves accept a 60 percent solution now; and embracing the possibility of nimbly flexing, adapting, and refining that solution as we learn new information.

Accepting "Not Knowing"

> In this increasingly complex world, it's impossible to see what's going on. The only way to see more of the complexity is to ask many others for their perspectives and experiences. Yet if we open ourselves to their differing perceptions, then we will find ourselves inhabiting the uncomfortable space of not knowing.
> —Margaret Wheatley, *Finding Our Way*

The skill of accepting "not knowing" acknowledges that we don't know all the answers, questions, facts, possible outcomes, contingencies, barriers, obstacles, or opportunities. It's about willingly embracing the discomfort of ambiguity and beginning to master the process of navigating through the unknown with courage and confidence instead of fear and insecurity. We as coaches master this skill by admitting that we don't know the outcome and willingly embracing the discomfort. We model this skill with our clients by engaging them in dialogue and exploring the many varied perspectives and experiences we collectively bring to the situation. In this way, we help them navigate "not knowing" with more confidence and less fear.

As we partner with our coaching clients to work on developing their mastery of aptly navigating complexity, chaos, and ambiguity, they will come face to face with the challenge of accepting that they don't know. They don't know all the answers, questions, facts, possible outcomes, contingencies, barriers, obstacles, or opportunities. The more we can assist our clients in realizing how much they don't know, the more they will realize how much more there is to know. Albert Einstein said it best: "As our circle of knowledge expands, so does the circumference of darkness surrounding it."

When we accept "not knowing" and willingly embrace the discomfort of ambiguity, we begin to master the process of navigating through the unknown with courage and confidence instead of fear and insecurity. We position ourselves to learn mastery of the practice of aptly navigating complexity, chaos, and ambiguity when we accept "not knowing."

Consider the following questions when coaching someone to accept "not knowing":

- What would happen if you acknowledged that you don't know?
- What is holding you back from inhabiting the uncomfortable space of not knowing?
- If you were to accept not knowing, what would be different for you?
- What opportunities are available to you to ask others for their perspectives and experiences?
- How could you effectively manage your feelings of discomfort as you step into the space of accepting not knowing?

BUILDING RESILIENCE

> Resilience is knowing that you are the only one that has the
> power and the responsibility to pick yourself up.
> —Mary Holloway

The skill of building resilience involves increasing one's capacity to recover or bounce back from difficulties and challenging circumstances. It means increasing one's ability to be elastic, flexible, and adaptable when facing stressful and demanding events. We master the skill of building resilience by shifting our mind-set about reality from viewing the world or our circumstances through an overly optimistic or overly pessimistic future frame to a staunch acceptance of our current reality. When we accept our present circumstances as they are and focus our attention and effort on managing our current reality, we refrain from unnecessarily depleting our energy reserves.

When our coaching clients choose to focus their agenda on strengthening their skill of building resilience, we can partner with them to explore their current mind-set and alternative possibilities that may serve them well in expanding their resiliency capacity. In her *Harvard Business Review* article "How Resilience Works" (2002), Diane Coutu writes, "Resilient people ... possess three characteristics: a staunch acceptance of reality; a deep belief, often buttressed by strongly held values, that life is meaningful; and an uncanny ability to improvise. You can bounce back from hardship with just one or two of these qualities, but you will only be truly resilient with all three."

We can start to build resilience by working on our mind-set about reality. If we gravitate naturally toward being overly pessimistic or overly optimistic, we may want to seek out ways to reframe our perspective of reality to one of pragmatically accepting our current circumstances. We know from the research on emotional intelligence that our emotions affect our thoughts. Although we cannot control what we feel, we can learn to make choices about what we say and what we do when we feel our emotions.

If we tend toward being overly pessimistic, we may experience feelings of being overwhelmed, anxious, fearful, threatened, or worried. Our pessimistic reaction could be one of the following:

- "It is what it is."
- "Why does this always happen?"
- "I don't see a way forward."
- "We'll never make it."
- "I can never do this right."
- "It's just the calm before the storm."

These pessimistic thoughts reinforce our initial feelings, and the reactive cycle continues. We expect bad things to happen, and then when they do, we feel validated in our expectations.

If, on the other hand, we tend toward being overly optimistic, we may experience feelings of hopefulness and confidence. Our optimistic reaction could be something like the following:

- "I know things look bleak at the moment, but I see light at the end of the tunnel."
- "Things can only get better from here."
- "This too will pass."
- "When life gives you lemons, make lemonade!"

These optimistic thoughts reinforce our initial feelings, and the reactive cycle loops. In many instances, we pull through without much difficulty or struggle, and our expectations are validated.

Coutu is saying that a staunch acceptance of reality is necessary if we want to build resilience. This means that if we can create a new mind-set of acceptance in contrast to pessimism or optimism, we can diminish the amount of energy that gets drained from unrealistic expectations and anticipation. When we learn to accept reality and regulate our emotions and behavioral responses, we conserve our energy for other activities. In the face of severe circumstances, we need all our energy to recover; if we are depleting it with a pessimistic or optimistic mind-set, we diminish our reserves for bouncing back.

Questions to consider when coaching someone to build resilience:
- What can you do to be kind to yourself?
- How can you support and nurture yourself?
- What strategies have served you well so far?
- What do you need to move beyond survival and thrive in this situation?
- What is your vision for the future?
- Who do you know that has built their resilience capacity, and how might you learn from their experience?

RESPONDING MORE, REACTING LESS

> When we get too caught up in the busyness of the world, we
> lose connection with one another—and ourselves.
> —Jack Kornfield

The skill of responding more and reacting less involves reacting less to fearful emotions and responding more with love. It's about accepting that we don't know all we wish we knew in the midst of complexity, chaos, and ambiguity. It means building our capacity to be elastic, flexible, and adaptable when facing stressful and demanding circumstances. We master this skill by responding more frequently to our encounters with complexity, chaos, and ambiguity with conscious intention and purposeful action. We practice accepting not knowing in the midst of complexity, chaos, and ambiguity, and we expand our resiliency capacity so that we can be flexible and adaptable when facing stressful and demanding circumstances.

When our coaching clients add learning the skill of responding more and reacting less to their coaching agenda, we can partner with them to explore how they are managing and regulating their emotions. Then we can partner with them to explore opportunities for applying this skill to learn mastery of the practice of aptly navigating complexity, chaos, and ambiguity.

Previously, in the chapter on authentic engagement, we learned that to dispel fear, we need to increase our emotional intelligence. When we react less to fear and respond more with love, we learn mastery in creating authentic engagement. We can also apply learning to respond more and react less to mastery of the practice of aptly navigating complexity, chaos, and ambiguity. By responding more frequently to our encounters with complexity, chaos, and ambiguity with conscious intention and purposeful action, we avoid depleting our energy reserves and build our capacity for resiliency. When we add the skill of accepting that we don't know, we have the tools we need to aptly navigate complexity, chaos, and ambiguity with less fear, anxiety, and insecurity.

Accepting "not knowing" in the midst of complexity, chaos, and ambiguity helps us move from a place of being overwhelmed into a place of calm and confidence. Instead of being distracted by voluminous data; confusing, conflicting, and competing priorities; and the lack of clarity, we find ourselves staying present and trusting our competence. When we learn to be comfortable with accepting "not knowing," we build our capacity for resilience and consistently react less and respond more. We are positioned to aptly navigate complexity, chaos, and ambiguity with acceptance and confidence.

Consider the following questions when coaching someone to respond more, react less:

- If you were able to reduce your impulsive reactions and increase your thoughtful responses, what would be different for you?
- What strategies would serve you as you embrace reacting less and responding more?
- What are your hot buttons that tend to trigger impulsive reactions?
- How have you managed these hot buttons successfully in the past?
- Who do you know that could serve as a role model or mentor?

We develop mastery of the fifth practice, "aptly navigating complexity, chaos, and ambiguity," by building on the previous four practices. First, we lay the foundation by fostering actionable trust. This involves extending, strengthening, and rebuilding trust in all our relationships. Second, we nurture authentic engagement by dispelling fear, fostering belonging, and cultivating courage. Third, we create a culture around aligned accountability by clarifying standards, holding everyone accountable to those standards, and providing performance feedback around those standards. Fourth, we encourage adaptive learning and mastery by embracing curiosity, adopting a beginner's mind, and embracing the concept of failing faster. Fifth, we develop mastery at being one who aptly navigates complexity, chaos, and ambiguity by accepting "not knowing," building resilience, and responding more and reacting less.

Aptly Navigating Complexity, Chaos, and Ambiguity Derailers

One enduring theme in derailment research by Ellen Van Velsor and Jean Brittain Leslie (1995) applies to aptly navigating complexity, chaos, and ambiguity:

1. **Inability to change or adapt during a transition**

   When leaders are unable to adapt to a particular boss or culture or when they have conflict with their upper management, they are at risk for the inability to change or adapt during a transition.

OPM's ECQ: Leading People and ECQ: Leading Change both have one derailer that applies to practice five:

1. **Competency: Conflict Management**
   - **Manages and resolves conflicts effectively**

     Leaders who struggle with effectively managing and resolving conflict frequently have to work harder at conflict management. Conflict avoidance is the most frequent strategy employed by leaders who struggle with this competency. When conflict is avoided, it escalates over time. Coaching leaders to develop mastery in conflict management and to step into conflict sooner will help mitigate this derailer.

2. **Competency: Flexibility**
   - **Adapts to organizational change**

     When leaders fail to adapt to organizational change, they often struggle with adapting to a boss, a new culture, or new mission priorities. Coaching leaders to accept that they don't know all they want to know at the time, helping them expand their resiliency capacity, and teaching them self-regulation skills helps mitigate this derailer.

   - **Is open to new ideas and opinions from others**

     Failing to be open to new ideas and others' opinions makes it difficult to navigate complexity, chaos, and ambiguity. Coaching leaders to strengthen their dialogue skills (covered in Practice Two: Authentic Engagement and the skill of fostering belonging) will help mitigate this derailer.

Use this checklist to identify potential derailment themes and behaviors you would like to work on in coaching. Check off those that may have been a challenge or a source of tension, or those that may benefit from further reflection and exploration.

Practice Five: Aptly Navigating Complexity, Chaos, and Ambiguity	Derailment Themes*	Derailment Behaviors*
❏ Accept "not knowing" ❏ Build resilience ❏ Respond more, react less	❏ Inability to change or adapt during a transition	❏ Unable to adapt to a boss ❏ Unable to adapt to a culture ❏ Conflict with upper management ❏ Strategic differences with management

* Derailment Themes adapted from *Themes in Derailment Research* (Van Velsor and Leslie 1995, Table 1). Derailment Behaviors adapted from *Themes in Derailment Research* (Van Velsor and Leslie 1995), OPM Leadership 360.

CHAPTER SUMMARY

Aptly navigating complexity, chaos, and ambiguity is the practice of accepting that we don't know all the answers, questions, data, circumstances, barriers, obstacles, or opportunities. It's about building resiliency so that we can bounce back from hardships and challenging circumstances. It's learning to intentionally respond more frequently and impulsively react less often in the face of complexity, chaos, and ambiguity. The practice is made up of the following skills:

- **Accepting "not knowing"**—the act of accepting that we don't know all the answers, questions, facts, possible outcomes, contingencies, barriers, obstacles, or opportunities. It's about willingly embracing the discomfort of ambiguity and beginning to master the process of navigating through the unknown with courage and confidence instead of fear and insecurity.

- **Building resilience**—the act of increasing one's capacity to recover or bounce back from difficulties and challenging circumstances. It's our innate ability to be elastic, flexible, and adaptable when facing stressful and demanding events.

- **Responding more, reacting less**—the act of reacting less to fearful emotions and responding more with love. It's about accepting that we don't know all we wish we knew in the midst of complexity, chaos, and ambiguity, and building our capacity to be elastic, flexible, and adaptable when facing stressful and demanding circumstances.

Crosswalk: OPM ECQs and Competencies and Practice Five: Aptly Navigating Complexity, Chaos, and Ambiguity

OPM ECQs and Competencies	Practice Five: Aptly Navigating Complexity, Chaos, and Ambiguity
ECQ: Leading Change This core qualification involves the ability to bring about strategic change, both within and outside the organization, to meet organizational goals. Inherent to this ECQ is the ability to establish an organizational vision and to implement it in a continuously changing environment.	
Flexibility: Is open to change and new information; rapidly adapts to new information, changing conditions, or unexpected obstacles.	• accepting "not knowing" • building resilience • responding more, reacting less
Resilience: Deals effectively with pressure; remains optimistic and persistent, even under adversity. Recovers quickly from setbacks.	• building resilience

RESOURCES

Books, Articles, Videos

Bennis, Warren, and Burt Nanus. 1997. *Leaders: Strategies for Taking Charge*. 2nd ed. New York HarperCollins.

Bradberry, Travis, and Jean Greaves. 2009. *Emotional Intelligence 2.0*. San Diego: TalentSmart.

Cherniss, Carey, and Daniel Goleman. 2001. *The Emotionally Intelligent Workplace*. San Francisco: Jossey-Bass.

Conner, Daryl R. 2006. *Managing at the Speed of Change: How Resilient Managers Succeed and Prosper Where Others Fail*. 2nd ed. New York: Random House.

Coutu, Diane. 2002. "How Resilience Works." *Harvard Business Review*, May.

Crum, Thomas. 2006. *Three Deep Breaths: Finding Power and Purpose in a Stressed-Out World*. San Francisco: Barrett Koehler Publications, Inc.

Flanagan, Tim, and John Lybarger. 2014. *Leading Forward: Successful Public Leadership amidst Complexity, Chaos, and Change.* San Francisco: Jossey-Bass.

Friedman, Edwin H. 2007. *Failure of Nerve: Leadership in the Age of the Quick Fix.* New York: Church Publishing, Inc.

Giguere, Miriam. 2014. "Tolerating Ambiguity—Being OK with Not Knowing." TEDxSoleburySchool, May 18.

Gino, Francesca, Todd B. Kashdan, David J. Disabato, and Fallon R. Goodman. 2018. "The Business Case for Curiosity." *Harvard Business Review,* September–October: 14.

Gladwell, Malcolm. 2005. *Blink: The Power of Thinking without Thinking.* New York: Little, Brown, and Company.

Goleman, Daniel. 1995. *Emotional Intelligence: Why It Can Matter More Than IQ.* New York: Bantam Doubleday Dell Publishing Group.

———. 1998. *Working with Emotional Intelligence.* New York: Bantam.

Goleman, Daniel, Richard Boyatzis, and Annie McKee. 2002. *Primal Leadership: Realizing the Power of Emotional Intelligence.* Boston: Harvard Business School Press.

Harris, Russ. 2013. *Getting Unstuck in ACT: A Clinician's Guide to Overcoming Common Obstacles in Acceptance and Commitment Therapy.* Oakland, CA: New Harbinger Publications, Inc.

Heath, Chip, and Dan Heath. 2017. *The Power of Moments.* New York: Simon and Schuster.

Joiner, William B., and Stephen A. Josephs. 2007. *Leadership Agility: Five Levels of Mastery for Anticipating and Initiating Change.* San Francisco: Jossey-Bass.

Pink, Daniel. 2018. *When: The Scientific Secrets of Perfect Timing.* New York: Penguin Random House LLC.

Quinn, Robert E. 1996. *Deep Change: Discovering the Leader Within.* San Francisco: Jossey-Bass.

———. 2004. *Building the Bridge as You Walk on It: A Guide for Leading Change.* San Francisco: Jossey-Bass.

Stein, Steven J., and Howard E. Book. 2011. *The EQ Edge: Emotional Intelligence and Your Success.* 3rd ed. San Francisco: Jossey-Bass.

Van Velsor, Ellen, and Jean Brittain Leslie. 1995. "Why Executives Derail: Perspectives across Time and Cultures." *Academy of Management Executive* 9 (4): 62–72.

Wheatley, Margaret. 2007. *Finding Our Way: Leadership for an Uncertain Time.* San Francisco: Barrett Koehler Publications, Inc.

———. 2010. *Perseverance.* Provo, UT: www.margaretwheatley.com.

Recommended Assessments

Coping and Stress Profile® (Inscape Publishing)
Measures your stress level for personal stress and work stress.
Measures four personal and four work coping resources: problem-solving, communication, closeness, and flexibility

Emotional Intelligence Appraisal® (Talent Smart)
Measures four skills: self-awareness, self-management, social awareness, and relationship management.

EQ-i 2.0 Model of Emotional Intelligence Leadership Report® (Multihealth Systems)
Four leadership dimensions: authenticity, coaching, insight, and innovation.
Five dimensions and fifteen subscales of EQ:

1. Self-perception (self-regard, self-actualization, emotional self-awareness)
2. Self-expression (emotional expression, assertiveness, independence)
3. Interpersonal (interpersonal relationships, empathy, social responsibility)
4. Decision-making (problem solving, reality testing, impulse control)
5. Stress management (flexibility, stress tolerance, optimism)

OPM Leadership 360 (United States Office of Personnel Management)
Measures the fundamental competencies and the five executive core qualifications (ECQs), including the twenty-two supporting leadership competencies.

viaEDGE® (Korn Ferry)
A self-assessment to provide insight into learning agility and assist in determining potential. It provides scores on five dimensions: mental agility, people agility, change agility, results agility, and self-awareness—and on overall learning agility.

CHAPTER 6

PRACTICE SIX:

Adroitness at Strategic Thinking

The process of creating strategy through critical reflection and dialogue in a continuous cycle of learning is what links it to excellent performance. It is the quality of this reflection and dialogue that makes a significant difference in the quality of strategic performance.

—Julia Sloan, *Learning to Think Strategically*

Michael began the coaching conversation with a check-in summarizing his progress and his experiences since our last meeting.

> Client: I've been using my breathing exercises much more frequently and applying them to a variety of experiences since we last met. Taking the time to pause, reflect, and intentionally take action has made a huge difference in the quality of my decision-making and in my mission contributions. As a result, my enthusiasm and optimism have increased too. I think this is all contributing to strengthening my resilience and tenacity as well.
>
> Coach: As you reflect on your progress, what comes to mind that would be important for you to explore today?
>
> Client: I'm making great progress with my own attitude and commitment to mission. Some of my relationships with my employees are improving. Performance and engagement are higher for a few that were lagging, and we all seem to have a deeper sense of comradery. Overall, I'm pretty satisfied. A few employees have shifted. I still have a couple who are lagging in performance and engagement. They don't act like they feel as if they are a part of the team. I'd like to talk about strategies for getting them engaged too.
>
> Coach: How would you like it to be different?
>
> Client: Ideally, I want everyone engaged and excelling in their work.
>
> Coach: What could you do to help make that a reality?

Client: I probably need to talk with them about it. Maybe they can tell me what they need to feel more engaged and to step up their performance.

Coach: When could you hold those conversations?

Client: Later this week would probably work. I will set up meetings when I get back to the office.

Coach: Is there anything else you need to talk about or identify before you have those meetings?

Client: I don't think so. I'd like to shift my attention and focus to strategy and customer relationships. My frustration seems to be focused on those two areas right now.

I don't know how to be strategic when tactical behaviors are the ones that get rewarded. When I try to be disciplined by applying quality decision-making and critical thinking to complex problems and mission requirements, my superiors get impatient. They want quick wins and immediate results. The ready-fire-aim approach is taxing. We fall into repetitive patterns of rework to fix unintended consequences and address missed mission requirements. I want to be able to influence my leadership by engaging them in dialogue and working toward collectively thinking and acting differently.

My customers are losing faith and confidence. I want to rebuild trust in these relationships before it's too late. This has to start with changing our approach internally. Once we learn to be more strategic and less tactical, I think our deliverables will be more aligned with our customer's needs and expectations.

Coach: What do you believe you need to shift to be more strategic and influential?

Client: I watched a TED talk by Simon Sinek called "Start with Why." He emphasized that leaders need to have clarity about their *why*, and they need to be able to articulate it in meaningful ways. He said *why* is about why you believe what you believe. When we're clear about what we believe and how our beliefs fuel our sense of purpose, meaning, and belonging, we can influence others to share our beliefs and want to become a part of what we are doing. Starting with my *why* seems like a good place to begin.

Coach: What is your *why*?

Client: I believe that what I do is a service to our country. As a public servant, I feel a responsibility to be a good steward of taxpayer dollars. Owning my piece of the agency's mission gives me the opportunity to take personal ownership of my contributions to preserving our way of life here in the United States of America.

Coach: As you hear yourself talk about your *why*, what emotions come up for you?

Client: My *why* gives me the opportunity to connect with a greater cause. Being a part of something greater than myself gives me a sense of belonging and purpose.

Coach: How will you take your learning about your *why* and move forward?

Client: First, I'm going to look for opportunities to share it. My next staff meeting would be a good place to start. I think it's also a good idea to share it from time to time in my one-on-one conversations with my employees. I know I need to share my *why* like I'm telling a story too. I've read in several books by authors like you, Brené Brown, Jim Loer, and others that the power of story is critical to keep in mind whenever I want to create a connection with others, especially when I'm talking about something important or meaningful.

Coach: What else do you need to know to be more strategic and influential?

Client: Well, once I've connected with others by telling my story and sharing my *why*, I'll have a better sense of who is in it with me. Then I can capitalize on the sense of belonging and shared ownership that will be generated by our shared *why*.

Next, I need to look at being less tactical and more strategic. As I get better at being strategic, my influence will expand with my leadership and my subordinates.

Coach: When you have become more strategic, what will you be doing differently?

Client: Again, I remember from *Leading Forward* (Flanagan and Lybarger 2014) that "Leaders who are competently adroit at thinking strategically skillfully juggle competing demands and incomplete information. They think beyond the immediate horizon, linking future objectives to current realities, and they inspire a clear, compelling vision of the agency's future." As I become more competent at thinking strategically, I'll be consistently doing these things.

Coach: What's your next step?

Client: First, I think that clarifying and articulating my *why* will help me inspire a clear, compelling vision. Second, I'll work on consistently using the pause strategy. If I take the time to stop, reflect, and link future objectives from our strategy to the current realities I'm facing, I'll be more effective at thinking beyond the immediate horizon.

Coach: What do you need to address to achieve that?

Client: I need to see the opportunities and remember to start with a pause. I recall another strategy from a leadership course I took. The instructor suggested that we can buy ourselves time for reflection by simply saying "I'll think about it" or "I need a few minutes to think about it first." I can put that into practice.

Coach: When you've learned to consistently clarify and articulate your *why* in an inspiring vision message and you've shown to link future strategic objectives to your current realities, what will be different for you?

Client: I'll be much more competent at thinking strategically! My confidence and optimism will be higher too.

Coach: What else is important for you to have to be fully competent at thinking strategically?

Client: The last thing for me is skillfully juggling competing demands and incomplete information. I go right to the details and get caught up in analysis paralysis. The more I dig into the competing demands by comparing risks and benefits, the more anxious I become about not making the best decision or making a wrong decision. My fear of missing something or getting it wrong paralyzes me.

Coach: How might you manage your fear and paralysis?

Client: Wow, once again, it's all about my breathing, isn't it? Remembering to breathe is the first step. I know I keep saying that my breathing is the key to everything, and it seems like I miss the connection over and over again.

I read in *Emotional Intelligence 2.0* that the author was pretty sure fish don't see water until they're out of it! It's the same with me and breathing. I don't see the relevance or connection of breathing to managing my anxiety and fear until I stop and change my breathing. When I'm taking in more breath, my emotions and my body shift.

Coach: We're coming to the end of our time together today. Is there anything else you'd like to talk about to bring closure to today's conversation?

Client: No, not for today, I think I have clearer direction and focus now. I know my next steps, and I'm committed to moving forward. Next time, I'd like to pick back up on influencing my superiors when they get impatient about not getting immediate results. I think by working on building my competence in thinking strategically, there'll be some impact on this area. I'd like to dig deeper, though, next time.

Coach: Before we end, would you summarize your action plan for the coming weeks?

Client: Sure. First, I will meet next week with my employees who are not fully engaged and find out what they need from me or their work to step up and fully contribute. Second, I will clarify and articulate my *why* in a clear, compelling story that illustrates my vision. Third, I will be more intentional about thinking beyond the immediate horizon by using the pause strategy. This will help me take the time to stop, reflect, and link future objectives from our strategy to the realities I'm facing.

Coach: Great! That sounds like a solid plan. Let's look at our calendars and set your next appointment.

Michael's Action Steps

1. I will meet next week with my employees who are not fully engaged and find out what they need from me or their work to step up and fully contribute.

2. I will clarify and articulate my *why* in a clear, compelling story that illustrates my vision.

3. I will be more intentional about thinking beyond the immediate horizon by using the pause strategy to take the time to stop, reflect, and link future objectives from our strategy to the current realities I'm facing.

MASTERING STRATEGIC THINKING

Being adroit at strategic thinking is the practice of developing mastery at thinking strategically. First, it's about knowing your *why*—that is, knowing why you believe what you believe. Second, it's about making quality decisions by incorporating dialogue. And third, it's about learning to juggle competing demands. We master strategic thinking by identifying why we believe what we believe about the mission and connecting that to our ability and opportunities to contribute to mission success.

Strategic thinking is about telling our story and actively seeking to understand others' through dialogue to surface hidden assumptions, expand possibilities, and broaden our perspectives. It's about improving the quality of our decision-making and learning to juggle competing demands and priorities, frequently in the midst of complexity, chaos, and ambiguity. When our coaching clients choose to focus their agenda on developing their ability to think strategically, it's important to guide them through an exploration of what strategic thinking is and how it's different from strategic planning.

Strategic thinking is often confused with strategic planning. A strategic plan is only as good as the strategic thinking that goes into it. Strategic planning is a systematic, linear process. Strategic thinking is a nonlinear, abstract process.

Julia Sloan defines strategic thinking this way in her book *Learning to Think Strategically* (2006): "Strategic thinking is a proposition that says we can affect the future through a strategic learning process that positions strategists as adaptive influencers in this ominously unpredictable environment rather than as victims or controllers." In his book *Deep Dive* (2009), Rich Horwath gives this definition: "Strategic thinking is the generation and application of business insights on a continual basis to achieve competitive advantage."

Strategic thinking mastery is developed by sharpening three skills:

1. Knowing your *why*
2. Making quality decisions
3. Juggling competing demands

Julia Sloan tells us in *Learning to Think Strategically* that when we create a strategy by applying critical reflection and dialogue in a continuous learning cycle, we link strategy to excellent performance, and we significantly improve the quality of strategic performance.

KNOWING YOUR WHY

> He whose life has a why can bear almost any how.
> —Friedrich Nietzsche

Wanting to know *why* starts in our early childhood years. We have insatiable curiosity about the world, people, and things that surround us. This need to know continues into adulthood. When we know why we do what we do—and why we believe what we believe—we can cultivate a sense of purpose and meaning about our lives and our contributions to work, family, and community.

The skill of knowing your *why* involves understanding why you believe what you believe and how that belief fuels your sense of purpose and meaning in life and work. Then you can tell your story in a way that communicates your values, strengths, and vision. We master this skill by clarifying our personal values, identifying our strengths, and creating our personal vision statements. Then we connect what we do at work, at home, and in our communities with our personal values, strengths, and vision.

When our coaching clients want to develop their skill at knowing their *why*, it's important to partner with them in clarifying their personal values, identifying their strengths, and creating a personal vision statement. The following are some tools to use in that effort.

VALUES CLARIFICATION EXERCISE

Using the Values and Definitions list in the Values Sort Exercise, identify those values that resonate with you as being important and influential in your life choices and decision-making. Think about your current place in work and in life. Your values can shift in priority and importance across the stages of your life and work. For this exercise, focus on the present. You might want to place a check mark next to those you select, or you may wish to highlight or underline them.

Values Sort Exercise

Values and Definitions

Achievement A sense of accomplishment, mastery, goal achievement	**Activity** Work under circumstances in which there is a high pace activity and work is done rapidly
Adventure New and challenging opportunities, excitement, risk	**Advancement** Growth, seniority, and promotion resulting from work well done
Aesthetics Appreciation of the beauty of things, ideas, surroundings, personal space, etc.	**Affiliation** Interacting with other people, being recognized as a member of a particular group, involvement, belonging
Affluence High income, financial success, prosperity	**Authority** Position and power to control events and activities of others

Autonomy Ability to act independently, with few constraints; self-sufficiency; self-reliance; ability to make most decisions and choices	**Balance** Giving proper weight to each area of a person's life
Challenge Continually face complex and demanding tasks and problems	**Change/Variety** Absence of routine; work responsibilities, daily activities, or settings that change frequently; unpredictability
Collaboration Close, cooperative working relationships with group or team members	**Community** Serving and supporting a purpose that supersedes personal desires; making a difference
Competence A high degree of proficiency and knowledge; showing above-average effectiveness and efficiency at tasks	**Competition** Rivalry with winning as the goal
Courage Willingness to stand up for one's beliefs	**Creativity** Discovering, developing, or designing new ideas, programs, or things using innovation and imagination; creating unique formats
Economic Security Steady and secure employment; adequate financial reward; low risk	**Enjoyment** Fun, joy, and laughter
Fame To become prominent, famous, well known	**Family** Spend time with significant other, spouse, children, parents, extended family, etc.
Fitness Maintaining physical fitness, strength, flexibility, cardiac health	**Friendship** Developing close relationships with others
Happiness Finding satisfaction, joy, or pleasure	**Health** Maintaining physical health and wellness, nutrition, diet
Help Others Helping people attain goals; providing care and support	**Humor** The ability to laugh at oneself and life

Influence Having an impact or effect on other people's attitudes or opinions; using the power of persuasion	**Integrity** Acting in accord with moral and ethical standards; honesty; sincerity; truth; trustworthiness
Justice Fairness, equality, doing the right thing	**Knowledge** The pursuit of understanding, skill and expertise; continuous learning
Location Choosing of a place to live (town, geographic area, etc.) that is conducive to one's lifestyle	**Love** Being involved in close, affectionate relationships; intimacy
Loyalty Faithfulness, duty, dedication	**Order** Respectful of authority, rules, and regulations; sense of stability, routine, predictability
Personal Development Dedication to maximizing one's potential	**Physical Fitness** Staying in shape—exercise and physical activity
Recognition Positive feedback and public credit for work well done; respect and admiration	**Reflection** Taking time out to think about the past, present, and future
Responsibility Dependability, reliability, accountability for results	**Self-Respect** Pride, self-esteem, sense of personal identity
Spirituality Strong spiritual/religious beliefs; moral fulfillment	**Status** Impress or gain other's respect by the nature and level of responsibility of one's job or association with a prestigious group or organization
Wisdom Sound judgment based on knowledge, experience, and understanding	**Wonder** Embracing curiosity; celebrating wonder and awe

Values Sort Exercise

This list is repeated from the Values and Definitions section. **Directions:** Rate each value by indicating whether you seldom or often value it.

Value	Seldom valued	Often valued
Achievement		
Activity		
Adventure		
Advancement		
Aesthetics		
Affiliation		
Affluence		
Authority		
Autonomy		
Balance		
Challenge		
Change/variety		
Collaboration		
Community		
Competence		
Competition		
Courage		
Creativity		
Economic security		
Enjoyment		
Family		
Fitness		
Friendship		
Happiness		
Health		
Help others		
Humor		
Influence		

Value	Seldom valued	Often valued
Integrity		
Justice		
Knowledge		
Location		
Love		
Loyalty		
Order		
Personal development		
Physical fitness		
Recognition		
Reflection		
Responsibility		
Self-respect		
Spirituality		
Status		
Wisdom		
Wonder		

Values Sort Exercise

Directions: Record your top three often-valued choices from the previous Values Sort exercise in the chart below. Describe how you live out these values.

Often Valued Values	Behavioral Examples
1.	
2.	

Often Valued Values	Behavioral Examples
3.	

STRENGTHS ASSESSMENTS

Buckingham and Clifton have written extensively about discovering our strengths. Two of their books that dive deeply into discovering and applying our strengths are *Now, Discover Your Strengths* (2001) and *Go Put Your Strengths to Work: 6 Powerful Steps to Achieve Outstanding Performance* (2007). Their online assessment, Strengths Finder 2.0®, gives users a summary of their signature strengths, identifies a person's unique sequence of thirty-four themes of talent, and shows people how to succeed by developing these themes into CliftonStrengths.

PERSONAL VISION STATEMENTS

There is something very powerful about putting our personal vision into written words and sharing them aloud. When we write it down, it makes it seem more real. When we publish it in our lives by taking a stand for what we believe, we fuel our passion, clarify our sense of purpose, and strengthen our connections with others.

I wrote my personal vision statement nearly twenty years ago. When I am considering new opportunities or evaluating new projects, I reflect on how they align with my vision and values. This helps me make wiser decisions about how I invest my time and effort.

John's Personal Vision Statement

I Can Make My Life Purposeful

I can make my life purposeful by transforming my talents into strengths. I believe I have unique talents, gifts, and abilities. These can be cultivated and grown into personal strengths. By discovering my strengths and mastering them, I can accomplish extraordinary things.

I can make my life purposeful by finding meaning in my work. When I play to my strengths—and do what I am the best at doing—I can achieve mastery. I believe that my life work can be filled with passion, excitement, and zeal.

I can make my life purposeful by being present in the world. When I build meaningful connections with people, I believe I create space for belonging in community, fellowship, stewardship, guardianship, and relationships.

I can make my life purposeful by studying my reflection in the mirror of my relationships. When I see myself in others—and learn how others see me—I have opportunities to choose between growth and stagnation. I believe I find purpose in my choices and the consequences that follow these decisions.

I can make my life purposeful by clarifying my values. When I am clear about my values and I live my life authentically—in alignment with my values—I find purpose in living, loving, and belonging.

I can make my life purposeful by asking powerful questions. When I am willing to ask hard questions, meaning arises out of uncertainty, clarity emerges from obscurity, order appears amid chaos, love conquers fear, and belonging replaces loneliness.

I can make my life purposeful. The choice is mine.

Personal Mission Statement

Live purposefully, love unconditionally, and belong in community.

Personal Values

- *Spirituality*—grow in faith, hope, love, grace, mercy, trust, and wisdom
- *Family*—support, encourage, and love my wife, children, and extended family
- *Relationships*—connect deeply; belong with others authentically, congruently, and genuinely
- *Autonomy*—celebrate independence, flexibility, innovation, risk-taking, and variety
- *Curiosity*—be open-minded, explore diversity, continuously learn and find humor, awe, and wonder everywhere

TELL YOUR STORY

When we change our stories, we change our lives—we change our experiences, and we change the consequences of our behaviors. Because we often believe that the stories we tell ourselves are the "truth," it's very challenging and difficult to change them! The first step is exploring our assumptions and beliefs about our experiences. The second step is changing our assumptions and beliefs to be more authentic and in alignment with our values. When we change our stories, we change our lives—we change how others perceive us—and we become more effective leaders.
—Tim Flanagan and John Lybarger, *Leading Forward*

When we are coaching our clients on developing the skill of knowing your *why*, we want to partner with them to explore how they might tell their stories in compelling, meaningful, and purposeful ways that not only inspire others to believe what they believe but that also make others want to join our clients to be a part of something bigger than themselves. Questions to consider include the following:

- What is the story you're telling yourself right now about your circumstances?
- How can you ground your story?
- How does your story serve you in this situation?
- Why do you believe what you believe about your current circumstances?
- What story do you want to tell?

MAKING QUALITY DECISIONS

> The discipline exhibited by good corporate decision makers—exploring alternative points of view, recognizing uncertainty, searching for evidence that contradicts our beliefs—can help us in our families and friendships as well. A solid process isn't just good for business; it's good for our lives.
> —Chip and Dan Heath, *Decisive*

The skill of making quality decisions involves practicing dialogue to explore alternative viewpoints; looking for data that challenges our mental models; and recognizing uncertainty, ambiguity, and chaos. It's ensuring that all stakeholders have a place and a voice at the table. It's creating a sense of personal and shared ownership in the decision-making process.

We master the skill of making quality decisions by practicing dialogue in all our decision-making meetings and ensuring that we explore alternative viewpoints, challenge our mental models, and recognize uncertainty. We include all stakeholders in decision-making meetings and activities. We create a sense of common purpose and shared ownership of the outcomes and deliverables.

When coaching clients want to add developing the skill of making quality decisions to their coaching agenda and action plan, we can partner with them to explore how they might include dialogue in their decision-making meetings. We can challenge them to commit to exploring alternative viewpoints, critically question mental models, and embrace uncertainty.

Questions to consider when coaching someone to make quality decisions include the following:

- What is another possibility?
- How might you see this circumstance differently?
- How do others see this circumstance?
- What additional information do you need to make a quality decision?
- Who else do you need to talk to before you make your decision?
- How will your decision impact others?

Juggling Competing Demands

> We pay attention to the mastery of technique and simultaneously focus on the overall form, the structure of a piece, changing emotions, and creativity. We learn to juggle many things at once, focusing and shifting our attention with ease.
> —Julia Sloan, *Learning to Think Strategically*

The skill of juggling competing demands involves identifying and managing demands that are critical to mission execution. It's learning to prioritize time, effort, and resources. It's learning to be agile and adaptable, and being able to realign and reprioritize in the midst of complexity, chaos, and ambiguity. We master the skill by learning to identify and prioritize competing demands for our time, effort, and resources. It's about learning to be agile and adaptable in the midst of complexity, chaos, and ambiguity. It's learning to shift and flex with resiliency, in the moment, without being constrained by fear or anxiety.

This skill isn't about juggling competing priorities that arise in our day-to-day routines. Those can be managed with traditional time-management tools. Juggling competing demands on mission priorities is a more complex challenge. Frequently our mission priorities shift for a wide variety of reasons. These can include new additions:

- partners
- stakeholders
- customers
- targets
- threats
- technologies
- leadership
- laws
- regulations, policies

When these new factors come into play, we must be able to juggle them without compromising our execution. The juggling requires nimbleness, flexibility, and adaptability. It's also influenced by our capacity for resiliency. Juggling drains our energy. Managing our energy and expanding our resiliency helps us master the skill of juggling competing demands.

When coaching clients want to add developing the skill of juggling competing demands to their coaching agenda and action plan, we can partner with them to explore their options and opportunities for learning to juggle, flex, and adapt in the moment without being constrained by fear or anxiety. Questions to consider when coaching someone to juggle competing demands include the following:

- If you don't juggle these competing demands, what would it cost you?
- In what ways would juggling these competing demands be beneficial to you?
- How can you juggle these various competing demands?
- If you were able to successfully juggle these competing demands, what would be different for you?
- What could you do differently to juggle these competing demands?
- How have you seen others successfully juggle competing demands?

Mastery of adroitness at strategic thinking is developed by building on the previous five practices good leaders master. First, we lay the foundation by fostering actionable trust. This includes extending, strengthening, and rebuilding trust in all our relationships.

Second, we nurture authentic engagement by dispelling fear, fostering belonging, and cultivating courage. Third, we create a culture around aligned accountability by clarifying standards, holding everyone accountable, and providing performance feedback. Fourth, we encourage adaptive learning and mastery by embracing curiosity, adopting a beginner's mind, and embracing the concept of failing faster. Fifth, we develop mastery at being one who aptly navigates complexity, chaos, and ambiguity by accepting "not knowing," building resilience, and responding more and reacting less. Finally, we can master adroitness at strategic thinking by first knowing our *why*, then learning to make quality decisions and juggle competing demands.

ADROITNESS AT STRATEGIC THINKING DERAILERS

One enduring theme in derailment research by Ellen Van Velsor and Jean Brittain Leslie (1995) applies to adroitness at strategic thinking:

1. **Inability to change or adapt during a transition**
   When leaders are unable to adapt to a boss with a different style, adapt to a different culture, think strategically, or struggle with making strategic decisions, they are at risk for the inability to change or adapt during a transition.

OPM's ECQ: Results Driven has one competency, decisiveness, with one derailer that applies to practice six:

1. **Competency: Decisiveness**
   - **Makes sound and timely decisions.**
     Leaders who fail to make sound and timely decisions are at risk for derailing. This behavior can lead to change resistance and avoiding taking timely action, and it can impair a team's ability to meet business objectives. Coaching leaders to develop mastery in adroitness at strategic thinking by developing the skills of knowing your *why*, making quality decisions, and juggling competing demands

Use this checklist to identify potential derailment themes and behaviors you would like to work on in coaching. Check off those that may have been a challenge or a source of tension or those that may benefit you with further reflection and exploration.

Practice Six: Adroitness at Strategic Thinking	Derailment Themes*	Derailment Behaviors*
☐ First, know your *why* ☐ Make quality decisions ☐ Juggle competing demands	☐ Inability to change or adapt during a transition	☐ Unable to adapt to a boss with a different style ☐ Unable to think strategically ☐ Difficulty making strategic decisions ☐ Unable to adapt to a boss ☐ Unable to adapt to a culture ☐ Does not make sound and timely decisions

* Derailment Themes adapted from *Themes in Derailment Research* (Van Velsor and Leslie 1995, Table 1). Derailment Behaviors adapted from *Themes in Derailment Research* (Van Velsor and Jean Brittain Leslie 1995), OPM Leadership 360.

CHAPTER SUMMARY

Adroitness at strategic thinking requires the following skills:

- **Knowing your why**—the act of knowing why you believe what you believe and how that belief fuels your sense of purpose and meaning in life and work. Then it's telling your story in a way that communicates your values, strengths, and vision.

- **Making quality decisions**—the act of practicing dialogue to explore alternative viewpoints; exploring for data that challenges our mental models; and recognizing uncertainty, ambiguity, and chaos. It's ensuring that all stakeholders have a place and a voice at the table. It's creating a sense of personal and shared ownership in the decision-making process.

- **Juggling competing demands**—the act of identifying and juggling demands that are critical factors in mission execution. It's learning to prioritize time, effort, and resources. It's learning to be agile and adaptable, and being able to realign and reprioritize in the midst of complexity, chaos, and ambiguity.

Crosswalk: OPM ECQs and Competencies and Practice Six: Adroitness at Strategic Thinking

OPM ECQs and Competencies	Practice Six: Adroitness at Strategic Thinking
Fundamental Competencies	
Public Service Motivation: Shows a commitment to serve the public. Ensures that actions meet public needs; aligns organizational objectives and practices with public interests.	• knowing your *why*
ECQ: Leading Change This core qualification involves the ability to bring about strategic change, both within and outside the organization, to meet organizational goals. Inherent to this ECQ is the ability to establish an organizational vision and to implement it in a continuously changing environment.	
Vision: Takes a long-term view and builds a shared vision with others; acts as a catalyst for organizational change. Influences others to translate vision into action.	• knowing your *why*
Strategic Thinking: Formulates objectives and priorities and implements plans consistent with the long-term interests of the organization in a global environment. Capitalizes on opportunities and manages risks.	• knowing your *why* • making quality decisions • juggling competing demands
ECQ: Results Driven This core qualification involves the ability to meet organizational goals and customer expectations. Inherent to this ECQ is the ability to make decisions that produce high-quality results by applying technical knowledge, analyzing problems, and calculating risks.	
Decisiveness: Makes well-informed, effective, and timely decisions, even when data are limited or solutions produce unpleasant consequences; perceives the impact and implications of decisions.	• making quality decisions

RESOURCES

Books, Articles, Videos

Bennis, Warren, and Burt Nanus. 1997. *Leaders: Strategies for Taking Charge.* 2nd ed. New York: HarperCollins.

Brown, Brené. 2017. *Rising Strong. How the Ability to Reset Transforms the Way We Live, Love, Parent, and Lead.* New York: Random House.

Buckingham, Marcus, and Donald O. Clifton. 2001. *Now, Discover Your Strengths.* New York: Free Press.

———. 2007. *Go Put Your Strengths to Work: 6 Powerful Steps to Achieve Outstanding Performance.* New York: Free Press.

Burgess, Tobin, Kevin Pugh, and Leo Sevigny. 2007. *The Personal Vision Workbook.* Thomson Delmar Learning.

Flanagan, Tim, and John Lybarger. 2014. *Leading Forward: Successful Public Leadership amidst Complexity, Chaos, and Change.* San Francisco: Jossey-Bass.

Harvard Business School Press. 2010. *Thinking Strategically: Expert Solutions to Everyday Challenges.* Boston: Harvard Business School Press.

Heath, Chip, and Dan Heath. 2013. *Decisive: How to Make Better Choices in Life and Work.* New York: Random House.

———. 2017. *The Power of Moments.* New York: Simon and Schuster.

Horwath, Rich. 2009. *Deep Dive: The Proven Method for Building Strategy, Focusing Your Resources, and Taking Smart Action.* Austin, TX: Greenleaf Book Group Press.

Kahneman, Daniel. 2011. *Thinking Fast and Slow.* New York: Farrar, Straus, and Giroux.

Olsen, Erica. 2006. *Strategic Planning for Dummies.* Hoboken, NJ: Wiley.

Sinek, Simon. 2009. *Start with Why: How Great Leaders Inspire Everyone to Take Action.* New York: Penguin Group.

Sloan, Julia. 2006. *Learning to Think Strategically.* Burlington, MA: Elsevier.

Van Velsor, Ellen, and Jean Brittain Leslie. 1995. "Why Executives Derail: Perspectives across Time and Cultures." *Academy of Management Executive* 9 (4): 62–72.

Recommended Assessments

Benchmarks 360® (Center for Creative Leadership)
Sixteen skills: resourcefulness, doing whatever it takes, being a quick study, decisiveness, leading employees, confronting problem employees, participative management, change management, building and mending relationships, compassion and sensitivity,

straightforwardness and composure, balance between personal life and work, self-awareness, putting people at ease, differences matter, career management

Strengths Finder 2.0® (Gallup)
Identifies a person's unique sequence of thirty-four themes of talent and shows people how to succeed by developing them into CliftonStrengths.

Decision Style Profile® (Discovery Learning/Multihealth Systems)
Measures five decision-making styles and five situational factors impacting decision quality, acceptance, and implementation.
- five styles: directing, fact finding, investigating, collaborating, teaming
- five factors: problem clarity, information, commitment, goal agreement, time

Everything DiSC Work of Leaders Profile® (Inscape Publishing)
Measures how you approach the most fundamental work of leaders:
- creating a vision: exploration, boldness, testing assumptions
- alignment: clarity, dialogue, inspiration
- execution: momentum, structure, feedback

EQ-i 2.0 Model of Emotional Intelligence Leadership Report® (Multihealth Systems)
Four leadership dimensions: authenticity, coaching, insight, and innovation.
Five dimensions and fifteen subscales of EQ:
1. Self-perception (self-regard, self-actualization, emotional self-awareness)
2. Self-expression (emotional expression, assertiveness, independence)
3. Interpersonal (interpersonal relationships, empathy, social responsibility)
4. Decision-making (problem solving, reality testing, impulse control)
5. Stress management (flexibility, stress tolerance, optimism)

OPM Leadership 360 (United States Office of Personnel Management)
Measures the fundamental competencies and the five executive core qualifications (ECQs), including the twenty-two supporting leadership competencies.

viaEDGE® (Korn Ferry)
A self-assessment to provide insight into learning agility and assist in determining potential. It provides scores on five dimensions: mental agility, people agility, change agility, results agility, and self-awareness, and on overall learning agility.

CHAPTER 7

PRACTICE SEVEN:

Audacious Pursuit of Mission Execution

Execution is the act of completing or finishing the job. Leaders are responsible for rallying those around them to carry out plans, implement actions, and accomplish goals. Performance counts. Results matter. Leaders embrace the mission and set examples for others to follow ... They support others in acting courageously while demanding accountability. Successful leaders get the job done without making excuses.

—Tim Flanagan and John Lybarger, *Leading Forward*

We began our coaching conversation by reflecting on Michael's learning to date.

Client: My commitments from our last conversation were to have conversations with my employees who still seemed to be lagging behind in performance and engagement. I also said I would look for opportunities to tell my story and share my *why* with my staff and our customers. And third, I committed to work on applying my breathing and pausing techniques to more skillfully juggle competing demands and incomplete information.

I had the one-on-one meetings with my employees that I was concerned about, and two went well. One was pretty challenging though. It seemed like it didn't matter what I said or how I tried to help, there was nothing but excuses and blame. I couldn't figure out how to get through and connect with him.

Coach: Tell me more about what happened.

Client: Well, he just kept saying that nothing could be done to improve things. He thinks he's tried everything to change the situation, and no one listens to him. All his ideas and suggestions have been met with resistance or refusals. He says that it just doesn't make sense to him to try anymore. I felt his resentment and bitterness were pretty deeply entrenched.

Coach: Do you think he's always been this way, or do you think something changed to create his current mind-set?

Client: I imagine something changed; it's hard to imagine that he was hired with this mind-set.

Coach: What could you do to influence his current mind-set?

Client: I could ask him what changed. Then I could explore it further with him and see if we could identify a path forward together.

Coach: How would you begin that conversation?

Client: First, I need to ask him what's changed and see if he's willing to tell me his story.

Coach: Then what would you do next?

Client: After I understand his story, I can look for ways to help him connect his *why* to what he does at work. I can also look for ways that I can encourage and empower him by supporting some of his ideas and suggestions. Maybe if he believes that I believe in him and will support him, his feelings just might shift.

Coach: What do you think he needs to be able to take this next step?

Client: He will need to trust me. I need to figure out how to extend and build trust with him so that he will consider risking and trying again.

Coach: Is there anything else you need to consider?

Client: No, I think that's a good start. I'll have another conversation with him before the end of this week.

Coach: What would you like to talk about next?

Client: Last time I ended our session saying that next time, I'd like to pick back up on influencing my superiors when they get impatient about not getting immediate results. I was confident that by working on building my competence in thinking strategically, there'd be some impact on this area, and it did make a difference. I'd like to dig deeper today.

I know we talked about this in an earlier coaching meeting, and I want to explore how I can find additional ways to connect my agency's various strategies execute mission priorities more effectively. This would help me identify more of their mission contributions and then give me opportunities to provide them with meaningful recognition. I've been doing some of this in connection with my employees' performance appraisals. Now I want to find ways to provide meaningful recognition on a regular and ongoing basis.

Coach: I'm delighted to hear you're continuing to make steady progress, Michael. As you reflect on the topics you just outlined as important to you to talk about, where would you like to begin?

Client: Developing my influencing skill is probably the most important for me to explore first.

Coach: When you've been successful at developing your influence skills, what will be different for you?

Client: Well, I think if I were more effective at influencing, I'd be more successful at persuading my supervisors and senior leaders to slow down and exhibit more patience. They'd listen to my appeals for dialogue, and we'd find the time to talk about our various mission priorities, customer needs, and expectations, and our current resources. If we did that consistently, I think there'd be less ready-fire-aim actions and more intentional, strategic actions, which would significantly reduce our rework and dramatically increase our critical mission effectiveness.

Coach: What do you believe you need to do to achieve more effectiveness at influencing?

Client: I think it ties back to our earlier conversation about clarifying and articulating my *why* and telling my story. I know in my head that emotions precede logic, and I consistently want to default to the logical rationale for taking a specific action. If I can pause and reflect and practice my breathing, I think I can identify the emotional drivers behind what I think is important to do or say as the next steps.

By taking a few minutes to pause and reflect, I can identify and articulate my feelings that are driving my beliefs about why what I think needs to be done should happen. When I'm able to articulate my emotions, I'll be able to tell a story that will appeal to the hearts as well as the minds of my supervisors and senior leaders. If I can capture their hearts by making a heartfelt and sincere emotional appeal, I'm confident their heads will go along and follow the logic too.

Coach: Is there anything else you might need to be successful at strengthening your influencing?

Client: I don't think so; it's just going to take practice and focused effort on my part.

Coach: What else is important for you to explore today?

Client: The other topic I wanted to be sure to cover today was exploring how I can more consistently connect my agency's various strategies to day-to-day actions. This will enable and empower my employees to execute mission priorities more effectively. Then I could clearly identify their mission contributions and provide them with more frequent meaningful recognition.

As I think about this, I realize that if I strengthen my strategic thinking and my influencing skills, this will happen almost automatically. I can use the power of story to share these connections in meaningful ways with my employees. When they share my belief in the *why* and take ownership of their own contributions to our mission, I'm confident they'll feel enabled to do their best work, and they will more likely be empowered to take the lead in their respective mission areas.

Coach: It sounds like you've made some important connections between your various personal goals. What else do you need to do to maximize your effectiveness in these areas?

Client: Providing meaningful recognition to my employees when they make significant mission contributions is important to me. I know that if my employees feel valued, appreciated, and recognized for their hard work, they'll be much more likely to be fully engaged and passionate about their work.

Coach: What would you be doing if you were successful at providing meaningful recognition to your employees?

Client: I'd know them well, and I'd understand their preferences for rewards and recognition. For example, I have some employees who would cringe at public recognition, and I have some that relish it. Some of my people like time off awards, and others prefer cash. Getting to know my people and their preferences for how they like to be recognized is an important investment for me to make in my people. Equally important is that knowing these things, I'd be able to be much more consistent at providing rewards and recognition.

Coach: Once again, we're nearing the end of our time together. Before we wrap up, is there anything unfinished for you today that we need to talk about?

Client: I feel good about my progress and the work we did together today. There isn't anything else I need to talk about at the moment.

Coach: You've covered a lot of ground over the past several months. As you reflect on the things that were important for you to explore in our coaching, how would you assess your progress to date?

Client: I'd like to take the next few days and work on a summary of my goals and progress that I've made on my leadership journey. I'd like to meet again at the end of the week and review it with you. Then we could talk about what would best serve me in terms of taking my learning forward.

Coach: That sounds like a solid plan to me. Before we close, would you summarize your action steps for the rest of the week?

Michael's Action Steps

1. I will have another conversation with my disengaged employee to seek to understand what's changed and what he needs to connect his *why* to his work.

2. I will continue practicing the pause-and-reflect strategy, taking a few minutes to identify and articulate my feelings that are driving my beliefs about why what I think needs to be done should happen. Then I can tell my story in a way that appeals to the hearts as well as the minds of my supervisors and senior leaders.

3. I will continue strengthening my strategic thinking and influencing skills so that I can more effectively and frequently provide meaningful recognition to my employees' mission contributions.

4. To further assist me in providing meaningful recognition, I will continue forging deeper relationships with my employees, and I will seek to understand their personal preferences for how they would like to receive meaningful recognition.

Coach: Thanks. Let's set up a meeting for next Friday morning!

Michael and John met the following Friday. Michael presented the following summary of his goals and progress.

Client: My three biggest questions when we started were: What can I do to improve my team's trust? How do I rekindle my first love for our mission so that I can remain engaged over the long haul? And is there a path forward amid the complexity, chaos, ambiguity, and constant change?

First, I worked on improving my team's trust. I started using four questions in each of our team meetings, and this has helped us extend trust and build deeper trust in one another.

Second, I worked on restoring my first love for public service. I learned that fear was the biggest obstacle. By practicing my breathing, I have been able to react less and respond more in situations that have historically been fearful for me. By learning to pay attention to my body and use my breathing to shift my emotions, I have been able to reduce fear and anxiousness, and increase my feelings of belonging and contentment.

Another important piece for me was learning to risk having difficult conversations to reduce conflict and improve performance with my team members. By stepping into conflict sooner, I don't have to work as hard and emotions don't escalate as much as they did in the past when I avoided addressing conflict.

Next, I worked on bringing clarity to my team around our agency's priorities, and how our team's goals align with them. This helped me identify contributions my team members were making to our mission successes, and I was able to more consistently recognize and reward their contributions.

My next goal was to work on adopting a beginner's mind to help me be open to curiosity. I saw again that my breathing was critical. Shifting my breathing shifts my emotions and moods. This helped me with my third question that I began with when we first met: "Is there a path forward amid the complexity, chaos, ambiguity, and constant change?"

My biggest insight was learning to hit the pause button. Stopping, thinking, and consciously choosing a response instead of impulsively reacting in the moment to the chaos and uncertainty also assisted me with building my confidence and comfort. I learned to increase my resiliency capacity by learning from my experiences; pausing and reflecting; impulsively reacting less, and intentionally responding more in challenging situations.

This has helped me be more thoughtful. I've been able to improve the quality of my decision-making and shift from being tactical to more strategic. Again, my breathing plays a critical role in shifting my feelings of anxiety and fear to enthusiasm and optimism.

Then I explored the concept of *why*. This helped me see that when I am clear about what I believe, and I am able to share my passion and purpose with others, it gives them an opportunity to decide if they share similar beliefs with me. When we are united around a common cause—a common belief—our engagement and productivity increases, and our mission results are positively impacted.

I learned that I can be more intentional about thinking beyond the immediate horizon by using the pause strategy to take the time to stop, reflect, and link future objectives from our agency's strategy to the current realities I'm facing.

I found that by engaging my employees in meaningful conversations about their personal *why*, I can help them find ways to reengage with the team and our mission. And when I use my story—my *why*—effectively, I can strategically influence my supervisor and senior leadership.

Finally, I was reminded that more than anything else, leadership is about relationships. As I continue to seek ways to forge deeper relationships with my employees, by seeking to understand their personal *why* and their preference for how they would like to receive personal, meaningful recognition, I become more effective with my strategic thinking and influencing skills.

Coach: You've put a great deal of thought and effective effort into your personal leadership development. Thank you for taking the time to comprehensively summarize and capture your learning, insights, and progress.

Is there anything unfinished for you that is important for us to explore together before we bring our coaching relationship to a close?

Client: No. I feel complete with our work. Thank you very much for partnering with me on this learning journey. I'm grateful for all that I have learned, and I feel confident about moving forward.

Coach: It's been an honor and my privilege to work with you as your leadership coach. I'm confident you will continue to grow and flourish in your leadership endeavors. Don't hesitate to reach back if I may assist you in the future!

MASTERING AUDACIOUS PURSUIT OF MISSION EXCELLENCE

The audacious pursuit of mission excellence is the practice of learning to connect our actions to strategy, then enabling others to fully engage in mission execution activities and consistently express meaningful recognition for team members' contributions to mission excellence. We master the audacious pursuit of mission excellence by learning three skills: seeking ways to connect actions to strategy, taking every opportunity to enable action, and seizing moments to give meaningful recognition.

Every public service agency has an important mission. Engaging and enabling employees to audaciously pursue mission excellence are critical steps that contribute to successful mission execution. When coaches partner with their clients in developing mastery in the audacious pursuit of mission excellence, they codesign and develop skill-building strategies that assist the client in connecting his or her job role responsibilities (actions) to the agency's strategic plan. When these connections are clear, employees are in a much better position to feel empowered, and they are enabled to action (mission execution). Providing meaningful recognition when employees make significant mission-area contributions helps reinforce their desire to continue pursuing mission excellence in their day-to-day activities.

CONNECTING ACTIONS TO STRATEGY

> When we default to tactical execution based on a drive for
> quick solutions, we waste precious resources.
> —Tim Flanagan and John Lybarger, *Leading Forward*

The skill of connect actions to strategy involves identifying the strategic actions that each employee is responsible for carrying out and connecting them with the agency's strategy for mission execution. We master this skill by shifting our mind-set from tactical execution to strategic execution. By focusing efforts on strategic execution, we preserve resources and create a culture in which employees feel fully engaged and clear about how their efforts contribute to mission success.

When your coaching clients choose to add developing the skill of connecting actions to strategy to their coaching action plan, it's important to partner with them to explore how to clearly define strategic actions for themselves and for their direct reports, and then align them with mission execution. Clients need to know and understand how critical these connections are for creating and sustaining employee engagement. Two critical employee engagement factors are knowing why you do what you do and knowing how what you do contributes to the agency's successful mission execution.

When coaching someone to connect actions to strategy, consider the following questions:

- You've identified your next steps; how do these connect to your overall goal?
- As you think about achieving your goal, what actions can you take to ensure success?
- How will you know when you have achieved your goal?
- What actions are critical to your successful achievement of your goal?
- What actions can you take to remove or mitigate the barriers or obstacles that could prevent you from executing your strategy?

ENABLING ACTION

> Leaders who enable and empower others to take action are the
> leaders who will succeed now and into the future.
> —Tim Flanagan and John Lybarger, *Leading Forward*

The skill of enabling action involves putting the right people in the right positions and empowering them to take strategic action aligned with mission execution. It's about building relationships with your people so that you can coach and mentor and guide them in their career development. It's about positioning your people for maximum engagement, contribution, and mission ownership.

We master the skill of enabling action by putting the right people in the right positions. Then we empower them to take strategic action aligned with the agency's mission. These steps require us to have or build relationships with our people so that we know them and develop mutual trust. Enabling actions strategically aligned to mission positions employees for maximum engagement, contribution, and mission ownership.

When coaching clients who have chosen to add developing the skill of enabling action to their action plan, it's important to help them explore how they can build trusting relationships and strategically align their own and their employees' actions to mission areas and activities. Consider the following questions when coaching someone to enable action:

- What do you need to move forward?
- When will you take your first step?
- When will you honor your commitment to yourself?
- What resources or support do you need to take action?
- What barriers are preventing you from taking action?
- What can you do to mitigate or remove those barriers?
- Who do you know that is effective at enabling action, and what can you learn from their example?

GIVING MEANINGFUL RECOGNITION

> When we recognize women and men for their contributions, we expand
> their awareness of their value to the organization and to their co-workers,
> imparting a sense of connectedness that, being social animals, all humans seek.
> While we may all be connected, leaders make sure that we're in touch.
> —James Kouzes and Barry Pozner, *Encouraging the Heart*

The skill of giving meaningful recognition involves personalizing and delivering recognition for employees' contributions in a way that is meaningful to the recipients. It creates a sense of connection and belonging—a belief that they are a part of something greater than themselves. We master the skill of giving meaningful recognition by learning and practicing the five languages of appreciation and the FAIR feedback method.

When your clients chooses to add developing the skill of giving meaningful recognition to their coaching agenda and action plan, it's important to partner with them in exploration of how to learn and apply the five languages of appreciation and the FAIR feedback method when giving meaningful recognition. Giving meaningful recognition to others is a skill that helps you, as a leader, contribute to making the recipient feel valued and appreciated. Our recognition of their efforts and contributions expands their awareness of how they are contributing to the mission and to their coworkers. We can foster belonging and a deeper sense of connection to the mission and to one another when we give meaningful recognition.

FIVE LANGUAGES OF APPRECIATION

In *The Five Languages of Appreciation in the Workplace* (2019), Gary Chapman and Paul White describe the five different ways in which employees prefer to receive recognition and appreciation. We each have a preferred language of appreciation. When we receive meaningful recognition from others expressed in our preferred language of appreciation, we consider it relevant and valuable. The languages are as follows:

1. *Words of appreciation*—affirming others either verbally or in writing. This can take the form of praise for contributions they have made, or it can be an affirming message about someone's character.
2. *Quality time*—giving another person your undivided attention. It can be done by joining others in quality conversations, shared moments, and small group dialogues.
3. *Acts of service*—with permission, offering assistance or support to accomplish tasks and assist others.
4. *Tangible gifts*—giving nonmonetary gifts to people who value them. This could include things like tickets for a sporting event, a movie, or a concert; a gift certificate for a restaurant; a card; or a small plant.
5. *Physical touch*—for example, a pat on the back, a handshake, a fist bump, or a touch on the hand, or on the arm. With some people, hugs are meaningful and appreciated. It's important, however, that we know and respect people's boundaries around physical space and physical touch.

The strategy for incorporating the five languages of appreciation is twofold. First, we need to learn our own language of appreciation and practice letting others know how we like to be recognized and appreciated. Then second, we can learn our coworkers' languages of appreciation and look for opportunities to give meaningful recognition in their preferred language of appreciation.

When you give meaningful recognition, you provide feedback that expresses appreciation for that person's or team's contribution. People value recognition and rewards when they are provided in ways that honor their contributions and acknowledge their efforts. Research has shown, too, that when people receive meaningful recognition, their trust in their leaders increases. In *The Leadership Challenge*, James Kouzes and Barry Posner share that when a leader is perceived as very frequently making it a point to let people know that he or she has confidence in their direct report's abilities, 70 percent of direct reports say they trust their leaders.

FAIR Feedback Method

The FAIR feedback method is also very effective for giving positive feedback that provides personalized recognition of effective effort. Coaches can use it with their clients and clients can use it with their colleagues. Here are some examples of what that feedback would look like.

Coach feedback to client

In our last coaching session, you committed to meet with your direct report and hold a difficult conversation about his past poor performance *(frame)*. You met with him as planned, and you reached agreement on a performance improvement plan *(action.)* I am pleased with your progress, and I am confident you will continue to have successes when holding difficult conversations as they arise, using the new skills you've learned to manage conflict *(interpretation)*. My request for you is that you find the courage to step into these difficult conversations promptly rather than delaying them. You will find that it takes less effort and work to resolve conflicts when you address them promptly *(request)*.

Client feedback to direct report

Amanda, I wanted to talk with you about the project you closed this morning *(frame)*. You met the project deadline, came in under budget, and exceeded our customer's expectations *(actions)*. I am proud of you, and I am pleased with your effective effort and results. I know I can count on you to lead and manage important projects. This last project had high visibility, and the director has been inquiring about some of the details because of our customer's high praise and compliments. Thank you for all the ways in which you help our division execute our mission and serve our customers *(interpretation)*. Will you promptly let me know if you have any future challenges or concerns so I can support you in addressing them *(request)*?

When employees are fully engaged, they are much more likely to take personal pride in and ownership of the agency's mission. Pride and ownership fuel the audacious pursuit of mission execution. Consider the following questions when coaching someone to give meaningful recognition:

- How could you learn what meaningful recognition looks like to your subordinates?
- What types of recognition are meaningful to your team members?
- How could you provide meaningful recognition to your team?
- How have you provided meaningful recognition in the past?

AUDACIOUS PURSUIT OF MISSION EXECUTION DERAILERS

One enduring theme in derailment research by Ellen Van Velsor and Jean Brittain Leslie (1995) applies to the audacious pursuit of mission execution:

1. **Inability to change or adapt during a transition**
   When leaders have strategic differences with their management, they are at risk for inability to change or adapt during a transition.

OPM's Organizational Impact has one derailer that applies to this practice:

1. **Leads without micromanaging**
   Leaders who micromanage their direct reports alienate their staff. The frequent unintended impact of this behavior is leaving the employee with the question, "Why am I in this job? If my boss can't trust me to do it and thinks I need micromanaging to be effective, why doesn't he/she do it him/herself or find a replacement for me who can?" Coaching leaders to know their people, to enable them to do their best work, and to provide meaningful, timely recognition for mission contributions will help mitigate this derailer.

Use this checklist to identify potential derailment themes and behaviors you would like to work on in coaching. Check off those that may have been a challenge or a source of tension, or those that may benefit from further reflection and exploration.

Practice Seven: Audacious Pursuit of Mission Execution	Derailment Themes*	Derailment Behaviors*
❏ Connect actions to strategy ❏ Enable action ❏ Give meaningful recognition	❏ Problems with interpersonal relationships ❏ Inability to build and lead a team ❏ Inability to change or adapt during a transition	❏ Insensitive to others ❏ Poor relationships ❏ Inability to build a team ❏ Inability to lead a team ❏ Failure to staff effectively ❏ Strategic differences with management

*Derailment Themes adapted from *Themes in Derailment Research* (Van Velsor and Leslie 1995, Table 1). Derailment Behaviors adapted from *Themes in Derailment Research* (Van Velsor and Leslie 1995), OPM Leadership 360.

CHAPTER SUMMARY

The audacious pursuit of mission execution involves learning to connect our actions to strategy, enabling others to fully engage in mission execution activities, and consistently expressing meaningful recognition for team members' contributions to mission excellence. It utilizes the following skills:

- **Connect actions to strategy**—the act of identifying strategic actions that each employee is responsible for carrying out and connecting them with the agency's strategy for mission execution.

- **Enable action**—the act of putting the right people in the right positions and empowering them to take strategic action aligned with mission execution. It's about building relationships with your people so that you can coach and mentor and guide them in their career development. It's about positioning your people for maximum engagement, contribution, and mission ownership.

- **Give meaningful recognition**—the act of personalizing and delivering meaningful recognition for an employee's contribution in a way that is meaningful to the recipient. It creates a sense of connection and belonging, and a belief that employees are a part of something greater than themselves.

Crosswalk: OPM ECQs and Competencies and Practice Seven: Audacious Pursuit of Mission Execution

OPM ECQs and Competencies	Practice Seven: Audacious Pursuit of Mission Execution
ECQ: Leading Change This core qualification involves the ability to bring about strategic change, both within and outside the organization, to meet organizational goals. Inherent to this ECQ is the ability to establish an organizational vision and to implement it in a continuously changing environment.	
External Awareness: Understands and keeps up-to-date on local, national, and international policies and trends that affect the organization and shape stakeholders' views; is aware of the organization's impact on the external environment.	• connecting actions to strategy • enabling action

ECQ: Results Driven This core qualification involves the ability to meet organizational goals and customer expectations. Inherent to this ECQ is the ability to make decisions that produce high-quality results by applying technical knowledge, analyzing problems, and calculating risks.	
Customer Service: Anticipates and meets the needs of both internal and external customers. Delivers high-quality products and services; is committed to continuous improvement.	• connecting actions to strategy • enabling action
Entrepreneurship: Positions the organization for future success by identifying new opportunities; builds the organization by developing or improving products or services. Takes calculated risks to accomplish organizational objectives.	• connecting actions to strategy • enabling action

RESOURCES

Books, Articles, Videos

Bossidy, Larry, and Ram Charan. 2002. *Execution: The Discipline of Getting Things Done.* New York: Crown Business.

Buron, Raoul J., and Dana McDonald-Mann. 1999. *Giving Feedback to Subordinates.* Greensboro, NC: Center for Creative Leadership.

Chapman, Gary, and Paul White. 2019. *The Five Languages of Appreciation in the Workplace.* Chicago: Northfield Publishing Empowering Organizations by Encouraging People.

Dive, Brian. 2008. *The Accountable Leader: Developing Effective Leadership through Managerial Accountability.* Bodmin, Cornwall: MPG Books Ltd.

Flanagan, Tim, and John Lybarger. 2014. *Leading Forward: Successful Public Leadership amidst Complexity, Chaos, and Change.* San Francisco: Jossey-Bass.

Govindarajan, Vijay, and Chris Trimble. 2010. *The Other Side of Innovation: Solving the Execution Challenge.* Boston: Harvard Business School Press.

Kouzes, James M., and Barry Posner. 2003. *Encouraging the Heart: A Leader's Guide to Rewarding and Recognizing Others.* Hoboken, NJ: John Wiley and Sons, Inc.

Loehr, Jim, and Tony Schwartz. 2003. *The Power of Full Engagement: Managing Energy, Not Time, Is the Key to High Performance and Personal Renewal.* New York: Free Press.

Van Velsor, Ellen, and Jean Brittain Leslie. 1995. "Why Executives Derail: Perspectives across Time and Cultures." *Academy of Management Executive* 9 (4): 62–72.

Wetzel, Sloan R. 2007. *Feedback That Works: How to Build and Deliver Your Message.* Greensboro, NC: Center for Creative Leadership.

Recommended Assessments

Leadership Practices Inventory® (LPI) (Jossey-Bass/Pfeiffer)
Measures five leadership practices and thirty leadership behaviors, six per practice.

1. **Model the way.**
   - I set a personal example of what I expect of others.
   - I spend time and energy making certain that the people I work with adhere to the principles and standards I have agreed on.
   - I follow through on the promises and commitments that I make.
   - I ask for feedback on how my actions affect other people's performance.
   - I build consensus around a common set of values for running our organization.
   - I am clear about my philosophy of leadership.

2. **Inspire a shared vision.**
   - I talk about future trends that will influence how our work gets done.
   - I describe a compelling image of what our future could be like.
   - I appeal to others to share an exciting dream of the future.
   - I show others how their long-term interests can be realized by enlisting in a common vision.
   - I paint the "big picture" of what I aspire to accomplish.
   - I speak with genuine conviction about the higher meaning and purpose of our work.

3. **Challenge the process.**
   - I seek out challenging opportunities that test my own skills and abilities.
   - I challenge people to try out new and innovative ways to do their work.
   - I search outside the formal boundaries of my organization for innovative ways to improve what I do.
   - I ask "What can I learn?" when things don't go as expected.
   - I make certain that I set achievable goals, make concrete plans, and establish measurable milestones for the projects and programs that I work on.
   - I experiment and take risks, even when there is a chance of failure.

4. **Enable others to act.**
   - I develop cooperative relationships among the people I work with.
   - I actively listen to diverse points of view.
   - I treat others with dignity and respect.
   - I support the decisions that people make on their own.

- I give people a great deal of freedom and choice in deciding how to do their work.
- I ensure that people grow in their jobs by learning new skills and developing themselves.

5. **Encourage the heart.**
    - I praise people for a job well done.
    - I make it a point to let people know about my confidence in their abilities.
    - I make sure that people are creatively rewarded for their contributions to the success of our projects.
    - I publicly recognize people who exemplify commitment to shared values.
    - I find ways to celebrate accomplishments.
    - I give the members of the team lots of appreciation and support for their contributions.

Everything DiSC 363™ for Leaders® (Inscape Publishing)
Eight approaches and twenty-four practices to effective leadership:
1. Pioneering (promoting bold action, stretching the boundaries, finding opportunities)
2. Energizing (showing enthusiasm, building professional networks, rallying people to achieve goals)
3. Affirming (being approachable, acknowledging contributions, creating a positive environment)
4. Inclusive (staying open to input, showing diplomacy, facilitating dialogue)
5. Humble (being fair-minded, showing modesty, maintaining composure)
6. Deliberate (providing a sense of stability, promoting disciplined analysis, communicating with clarity)
7. Resolute (improving methods, speaking up about problems, setting high expectations)
8. Commanding (focusing on results, taking charge, showing confidence)

OPM Leadership 360 (US Office of Personnel Management)
Measures the fundamental competencies and the five executive core qualifications (ECQs), including the twenty-two supporting leadership competencies.

CHAPTER 8

Leader Development and Action Planning

The most dangerous leadership myth is that leaders are born—that there is a genetic factor to leadership. This myth asserts that people simply either have certain charismatic qualities or not. That's nonsense; in fact, the opposite is true. Leaders are made rather than born. And the way we become leaders is by learning about leadership through life and job experiences, not with university degrees.

—Warren G. Bennis, *Managing People Is Like Herding Cats*

LEADER DEVELOPMENT ACTION PLANNING

This worksheet and resource section may be used by both internal and external coaches to guide the formulation of a leader development action plan. Putting a plan in writing, sharing it with another person, and asking for accountability are all steps that significantly improve the probability of successful action-plan execution.

Have your clients write out the plan; don't prepare it for them. This step helps to create personal accountability and buy-in for the action plan. In your role as coach, partner with your client to cocreate his or her goals. Remember to let the client drive this process. The client owns and creates the action plan, not the coach. The coach may make suggestions or recommendations for resources and/or may function as an accountability partner if the client makes a request.

LEADER DEVELOPMENT ACTION PLAN WORKSHEET

Name: _____ **Date:** _____/_____/_____

Instructions

Record your goals. It is recommended that you limit your goals to a maximum of three. When people set multiple goals, they have a tendency to get overwhelmed and fail to execute any of them. For each goal, indicate the practice good leaders master for which the goal aligns.

1. **Actionable trust**
   - Extend trust.
   - Strengthen trust.
   - Rebuild trust,

2. **Authentic engagement**
   - Dispel fear.
   - Foster belonging.
   - Cultivate courage.

3. **Aligned accountability**
   - Clarify standards.
   - Hold everyone accountable.
   - Provide direct feedback.

4. **Adaptive learning and mastery**
   - Embrace curiosity.
   - Adopt a beginner's mind.
   - Fail faster.

5. **Aptly navigating complexity, chaos, and ambiguity**
   - Accept "not knowing."
   - Build resilience.
   - Respond more, react less.

6. **Adroitness at strategic thinking**
   - First, know your *why*.
   - Make quality decisions.
   - Juggle competing demands.

7. **Audacious Pursuit of Mission Execution**
   - Connect actions to strategy.
   - Enable action.
   - Give meaningful recognition.

Review the seven practices good leaders master and the derailment themes and behaviors checklist. Incorporate any identified derailment behaviors into your development goals.

Consider a combination of short-term, intermediate, and long-term goals as you prepare your Leader Development Action Plan Worksheet. This helps you prioritize and plan your action steps more efficiently. Where possible, use the SMART approach to goal writing. SMART goals are defined as follows:

- *Specific*—Describe goal in behavioral terms: what will you say or do?
- *Measurable*—Quantify your actions (e.g., number of hours, days, people, meetings).
- *Achievable*—Describe how you will take specific action(s) identified in your goal.
- *Results-focused*—Describe the result, outcome, or deliverable you expect to achieve.
- *Time-bound*—Identify time (day, month, year) in which you will complete the action(s).

Examples

Goal #1
Practice Alignment: Actionable Trust

I will strengthen trust with my subordinate, John Doe, by scheduling three one-on-one, face-to-face, weekly meetings with him on Mondays at 8:30 a.m., starting next week. During these meetings, I will listen deeply, ask powerful questions, seek to understand his *why*, and inquire about what he would like to do to align his purpose and passion with his current position. I will partner with him to maximize his engagement.

Goal #2
Practice Alignment: Audacious Pursuit of Mission Execution

I will give formal, meaningful recognition to my three direct reports during each of my feedback meetings at the end of this current performance-review cycle. Additionally, I will give informal, meaningful recognition to my three direct reports on a weekly basis, in ways that are personally meaningful to them, beginning next week and continuing for the next ninety days.

For each goal, describe the action steps you plan to implement. Write these steps in behavioral terms, describing what you will do and what you will say to successfully execute each step. Identify the resources you will need to successfully achieve each goal. This can include things like books, articles, videos, assessments, budget, or any other items you identify as essential for your goal attainment. Finally, identify the types of support you anticipate you will need for each goal. This can include accountability partner(s), mentor(s), coach, supervisor, colleague(s), or anyone else you identify as critical for your goal achievement.

Leader Development Goals and Action Steps:

Goal #1
Practice Alignment: _____

_____
_____
_____
_____
_____
_____

Action Steps

_____
_____
_____
_____
_____
_____
_____
_____

Needed Resources
(Books, articles, videos, assessments, budget)

_____
_____
_____
_____
_____
_____
_____

Needed Support
(Accountability partner, mentor, coach, supervisor, colleague)

_____
_____
_____
_____
_____
_____
_____

Goal #2

Practice Alignment: _____

_____

_____

_____

_____

_____

_____

Action Steps

_____

_____

_____

_____

_____

_____

_____

_____

Needed Resources

(Books, articles, videos, assessments, budget)

_____

_____

_____

_____

_____

_____

_____

Needed Support

(Accountability partner, mentor, coach, supervisor, colleague)

_____

_____

_____

_____

_____

_____

_____

_____

Goal #3
Practice Alignment: _____

_____

_____

_____

_____

_____

_____

Action Steps

_____

_____

_____

_____

_____

_____

_____

_____

Needed Resources
(Books, articles, videos, assessments, budget)

_____

_____

_____

_____

_____

_____

_____

Needed Support
(Accountability partner, mentor, coach, supervisor, colleague)

_____

_____

_____

_____

_____

_____

_____

CHAPTER 9

Coach Development and Action Planning

Coaching is partnering with clients in a thought-provoking and creative process that inspires them to maximize their personal and professional potential.

—International Coach Federation

This chapter focuses on developing coaching competence. The tools and resources may be used by anyone who wants to develop his or her coaching skills. Employees who want to improve their coaching skills as part of their leader development will find great benefit in using and applying these resources. Coaches who want to improve their core coaching competence mastery will find these resources very practical and applicable to their development journey too.

COACH DEVELOPMENT ACTION PLANNING

This section is designed for developing coaching competence. It includes the ICF coaching definition and the ICF core coaching competencies. Coaches can also reference the ICF code of ethics in the appendix.

ICF COACHING DEFINITION*

Coaching is partnering with clients in a thought-provoking and creative process that inspires them to maximize their personal and professional potential.

ICF CORE COACHING COMPETENCIES*

The eleven ICF Core Competencies are grouped into four clusters according to those that fit together logically based on common ways of looking at the competencies in each group.

The groupings and individual competencies are not weighted—they do not represent any kind of priority in that they are all core or critical for any competent coach to demonstrate.

Cluster #1: Setting the Foundation
1. Meeting ethical guidelines and professional standards
2. Establishing the coaching agreement

Cluster #2: Cocreating the Relationship
3. Establishing trust and intimacy with the client
4. Coaching presence

Cluster #3: Communicating Effectively
5. Active listening
6. Powerful questioning
7. Direct communication

Cluster #4: Facilitating Learning and Results
8. Creating awareness
9. Designing actions
10. Planning and goal-setting
11. Managing progress and accountability

*Reprinted with permission, International Coach Federation.

International Coach Federation (ICF) PCC Markers

Assessment markers are the indicators that an assessor is trained to listen for and determine which ICF core competencies are in evidence in a recorded coaching conversation, and to what extent. The following markers are the behaviors that should be exhibited in a coaching conversation at the professional certified coach (PCC) level. These markers support a performance evaluation process that is fair, consistent, valid, reliable, repeatable, and defensible. Please note these markers are not a tool for coaching and should not be used as a checklist or formula for passing the performance evaluation.

Competency 2: Creating the Coaching Agreement

1. Coach helps the client identify, or reconfirm, what s/he wants to accomplish in the session.
2. Coach helps the client to define or reconfirm measures of success for what s/he wants to accomplish in the session.
3. Coach explores what is important or meaningful to the client about what s/he wants to accomplish in the session.
4. Coach helps the client define what the client believes he/she needs to address or resolve in order to achieve what s/he wants to accomplish in the session.

5. Coach continues conversation in direction of client's desired outcome unless client indicates otherwise.

COMPETENCY 3: CREATING TRUST AND INTIMACY

1. Coach acknowledges and respects the client's work in the coaching process.
2. Coach expresses support for the client.
3. Coach encourages and allows the client to fully express him/herself.

COMPETENCY 4: COACHING PRESENCE

1. Coach acts in response to both the whole person of the client and what the client wants to accomplish in the session.
2. Coach is observant, empathetic, and responsive.
3. Coach notices and explores energy shifts in the client.
4. Coach exhibits curiosity with the intent to learn more.
5. Coach partners with the client by supporting the client to choose what happens in the session.
6. Coach partners with the client by inviting the client to respond in any way to the coach's contributions and accepts the client's response.
7. Coach partners with the client by playing back the client's expressed possibilities for the client to choose from.
8. Coach partners with the client by encouraging the client to formulate his or her own learning.

COMPETENCY 5: ACTIVE LISTENING

1. Coach's questions and observations are customized by using what the coach has learned about who the client is and the client's situation.
2. Coach inquires about or explores the client's use of language.
3. Coach inquires about or explores the client's emotions.
4.

inflection as appropriate.
5. Coach inquires about or explores the client's behaviors.
6. Coach inquires about or explores how the client perceives his/her world.
7. Coach is quiet and gives client time to think.

COMPETENCY 6: POWERFUL QUESTIONING

1. Coach asks questions about the client; his/her way of thinking, assumptions, beliefs, values, needs, wants, etc.
2. Coach's questions help the client explore beyond his/her current thinking to new or expanded ways of thinking about himself/herself.

3. Coach's questions help the client explore beyond his/her current thinking to new or expanded ways of thinking about his/her situation.
4. Coach's questions help the client explore beyond current thinking toward the outcome s/he desires.
5. Coach asks clear, direct, primarily open-ended questions, one at a time, at a pace that allows for thinking and reflection by the client.
6. Coach's questions use the client's language and elements of the client's learning style and frame of reference.
7. Coach's questions are not leading (i.e., do not contain a conclusion or direction).

COMPETENCY 7: DIRECT COMMUNICATION

1. Coach shares observations, intuitions, comments, thoughts and feelings to serve the client's learning or forward movement.
2. Coach shares observations, intuitions, comments, thoughts, and feelings without any attachment to them being right.
3. Coach uses the client's language or language that reflects the client's way of speaking.
4. Coach's language is generally clear and concise.
5. The coach allows the client to do most of the talking.
6. Coach allows the client to complete speaking without interrupting unless there is a stated coaching purpose to do so.

COMPETENCY 8: CREATING AWARENESS

1. Coach invites client to state and/or explore his/her learning in the session about her/his situation (the what).
2. Coach invites client to state and/or explore his/her learning in the session about her-/himself (the who).
3. Coach shares what s/he is noticing about the client and/or the client's situation, and seeks the client's input or exploration.
4. Coach invites client to consider how s/he will use new learning from the coaching.
5. Coach's questions, intuitions, and observations have the potential to create new learning for the client.

COMPETENCY 9, 10, AND 11: DESIGNING ACTIONS, PLANNING AND GOAL SETTING, AND MANAGING PROGRESS AND ACCOUNTABILITY

1. Coach invites or allows client to explore progress toward what s/he want to accomplish in the session.
2. Coach assists the client to design what actions/thinking client will do after the session in order for the client to continue moving toward the client's desired outcomes.

3. Coach invites or allows client to consider her/his path forward, including, as appropriate, support mechanisms, resources, and potential barriers.
4. Coach assists the client to design the best methods of accountability for her-/himself.
5. Coach partners with the client to close the session.
6. Coach notices and reflects client's progress.

Reprinted with permission, International Coach Federation.

COACH DEVELOPMENT ACTION PLAN WORKSHEET

Coach Development Action Plan Worksheet

Name: _____ **Date:** _____/_____/_____

Instructions

First, record your goals. It is strongly recommended that you limit your goals to a maximum of three at a time. When people set multiple goals, they have a tendency to get overwhelmed and fail to execute any. For each goal, indicate the ICF core coaching competency to which the goal aligns. Consider a combination of short-term, intermediate, and long-term goals as you prepare your Coach Development Action Plan Worksheet. This helps you prioritize and plan your action steps more efficiently.

Second, where possible, use the SMART approach to goal writing. SMART goals are defined as follows:

- *Specific*—Describe goal in behavioral terms, what will you say or do?
- *Measurable*—Quantify your actions (e.g., number of hours, days, people, meetings).
- *Action-oriented*—Describe how you will take specific action(s) identified in your goal.
- *Results-focused*—Describe the result, outcome, or deliverable you expect to achieve.
- *Time-bound*—Identify time (day, month, year) in which you will complete the action(s).

The following are examples of properly stated goals:

Goal #1
ICF Core Coaching Competency: Establishing the Coaching Agreement

Starting with my next coaching session, I will begin each session by inviting the client to clearly identify what the client wants to address in the session. I will explore what is important and meaningful to the client about desired goals. I will partner with the client to define what needs to be addressed or resolve in order to achieve what the client wants in the session.

Goal #2:
ICF Core Coaching Competency: Direct Communication

After I complete fifteen more hours of coaching practice, during each coaching session, I will ask clear, direct questions, one at a time. I will not layer questions. I will incorporate the client's language, metaphors, or analogies to personalize my communication and positively impact the client.

Third, for each goal, describe the action steps you plan to implement to successfully complete your goal. Write these action steps in behavioral terms, describing what you will do and what you will say to successfully execute each step.

Fourth, for each goal, identify the resources you will need to successfully achieve your goal. This can include things like books, articles, videos, assessments, budget, mentor coaching, coach specific training, or any other items you identify as essential for your goal attainment.

Fifth, for each goal, identify the types of support you anticipate you will need. This can include accountability partner(s), mentor(s), coach, supervisor, colleague(s), or anyone else you identify as critical for your goal achievement.

Coach Development Goals and Action Steps

Goal #1
ICF Core Coaching Competency: _____

_____
_____
_____
_____
_____
_____

Action Steps

_____
_____
_____
_____
_____
_____
_____
_____

Needed Resources
(Books, articles, videos, assessments, budget)

_____
_____
_____
_____
_____
_____
_____

Needed Support
(Accountability partner, mentor coach, coach, colleague)

_____
_____
_____
_____
_____
_____
_____

Goal #2

ICF Core Coaching Competency: _____

_____

_____

_____

_____

_____

_____

Action Steps

_____

_____

_____

_____

_____

_____

_____

_____

Needed Resources

(Books, articles, videos, assessments, budget)

_____

_____

_____

_____

_____

_____

_____

_____

Needed Support

(Accountability partner, mentor coach, coach, colleague)

_____

_____

_____

_____

_____

_____

_____

_____

Goal #3
ICF Core Coaching Competency: _____

_____
_____
_____
_____
_____
_____
_____

Action Steps

_____
_____
_____
_____
_____
_____
_____
_____
_____

Needed Resources
(Books, articles, videos, assessments, budget)

_____
_____
_____
_____
_____
_____
_____
_____

Needed Support
(Accountability partner, mentor coach, coach, colleague)

_____
_____
_____
_____
_____
_____
_____
_____
_____

RESOURCES

Books, Articles, Videos

Atkins, Andy. 2012. "How Leaders Build Trust." *Fast Company*, August 7. http://www.fastcompany.com/3000204/how-leaders-build-trust.

Bennis, Warren, and Burt Nanus. 1997. *Leaders: Strategies for Taking Charge.* 2nd ed. New York: HarperCollins.

Bishop, Scott R., Mark Lau, Shauna L. Shapiro, Linda Carlson, Nicole D. Anderson, James Carmody, and Gerald Devins. 2004. "Mindfulness: A Proposed Operational Definition." *Clinical Psychology: Science and Practice*, 11: 230–241.

Blanchard, Ken, Patricia Zigarmi, and Drea Zigarmi. 1985. *Leadership and the One Minute Manager: Increasing Effectiveness through Situational Leadership.* New York: Morrow.

Block, Peter. 1987. *The Empowered Manager: Positive Political Skills at Work.* San Francisco: Jossey-Bass.

Boser, Ulrich. 2018. "Learning is a Learned Behavior. Here's How to Get Better at It." *Harvard Business Review*, May 2.

Bossidy, Larry, and Ram Charan. 2002. *Execution. The Discipline of Getting Things Done.* New York: Crown Business.

Bradberry, Travis, and Jean Greaves. 2009. *Emotional Intelligence 2.0.* San Diego: TalentSmart.

Brandon, Rick, and Marty Seldman. 2004. *Survival of the Savvy. High-Integrity Political Tactics for Career and. Company Success.* New York: Free Press.

Bregman, Peter. 2016. "The Right Way to Hold People Accountable." *Harvard Business Review*, January 11.

Brown, Brené. 2017. *Braving the Wilderness. The Quest for True Belonging and the Courage to Stand Alone.* New York: Random House.

———. 2017. *Rising Strong. How the Ability to Reset Transforms the Way We Live, Love, Parent, and Lead.* New York: Random House.

———. 2018. *Dare to Lead: Brave Work. Tough Conversations. Whole Hearts.* New York: Random House.

Brown, Shona L., and Kathleen M. Eisenhardt. 1998. *Competing on the Edge: Strategy as Structured Chaos.* Boston: Harvard Business School Press.

Buckingham, Marcus. 2007. *Go Put Your Strengths to Work: 6 Powerful Steps to Achieve Outstanding Performance.* New York: Free Press.

Buckingham, Marcus, and Donald O. Clifton. 2001. *Now, Discover Your Strengths.* New York: Free Press.

Burgess, Tobin, Kevin Pugh, and Leo Sevigny. 2007. *The Personal Vision Workbook.* Thomson Delmar Learning.

Buron, Raoul J., and Dana McDonald-Mann. 1999. *Giving Feedback to Subordinates.* Greensboro, NC: Center for Creative Leadership.

Carlin, John. 2008. *Playing the Enemy: Nelson Mandela and the Game that Made a Nation.* New York: Penguin Press.

Carpenter, M. Scott, L. Gordon Cooper, John. H. Glenn Jr., Virgil I. Grissom, Walter M. Schirra Jr., Alan B. Shepard, and Donald K. Slayton. 1962. *We Seven.* New York: Simon and Schuster.

Chapman, Gary, and Paul White. 2019. *The Five Languages of Appreciation in the Workplace.* Chicago: Northfield Publishing Empowering Organizations by Encouraging People.

Cherniss, Carey, and Daniel Goleman. 2001. *The Emotionally Intelligent Workplace.* San Francisco: Jossey-Bass.

Conner, Daryl. R. 2006. *Managing at the Speed of Change: How Resilient Managers Succeed and Prosper Where Others Fail.* 2nd ed. New York: Random House.

Cottrell, David. 2002. *Monday Morning Leadership: 8 Mentoring Sessions You Can't Afford to Miss.* Dallas: Cornerstone Leadership Institute.

Coutu, Diane. 2002. "How Resilience Works." *Harvard Business Review,* May Issue.

Covey, Stephen M. R. 2018. *The Speed of Trust: The One Thing That Changes Everything.* New York: Free Press.

Covey, Stephen R. 2004. *The Seven Habits of Highly Effective People: Powerful Lessons in Personal Change.* New York: Simon and Shuster.

Crum, Thomas. 2006. *Three Deep Breaths: Finding Power and Purpose in a Stressed-Out World.* San Francisco: Barrett Koehler Publications, Inc.

DeBecker, Gavin. 1999. *The Gift of Fear: This Book Can Save Your Life and Other Survival Signals That Protect Us from Violence.* New York: Dell Publishing.

Deluca, Joel R. 1999. *Political Savvy: Systematic Approaches to Leadership Behind-the-Scenes.* Pittsburgh: EBG Publications.

Dethmer, Jim, Diana Chapman, and Kaley Warner Klemp. 2014. *The 15 Commitments of Conscious Leadership.* KaleyKlemp.com.

Dive, Brian. 2008. *The Accountable Leader: Developing Effective Leadership through Managerial Accountability.* Bodmin, Cornwall: MPG Books Ltd.

Dixit, Avinash, and Barry J. Nalebuff. 2008. *The Art of Strategy: A Game Theorist's Guide to Success in Business and Life.* New York: Norton.

Dweck, Carol S. 2016. *Mindset: The New Psychology of Success: How We Can Learn to Fulfill Our Potential.* New York: Ballantine Books.

Eblin, Scott. 2011. *The Next Level: What Insiders Know about Executive Success.* 2nd ed. Boston: Nicholas Brealey Publishing.

Edmondson, Amy C. 2004. "Psychological Safety, Trust, and Learning in Organizations: A Group-Level Lens." In *Trust and Distrust in Organizations*, edited by Roderick Kramer and Karen Cook. New York: Russell Sage Foundation.

Feltman, C. 2009. *The Thin Book of Trust: An Essential Primer for Building Trust at Work.* Bend, OR: Thin Book Publishing.

Ferris, Gerald. R., Sherry L. Davidson, and Pamela L. Perrewe. 2005. *Political Skill at Work: Impact on Work Effectiveness.* Boston: Davies-Black.

Flanagan, Tim, and John Lybarger. 2014. *Leading Forward: Successful Public Leadership amidst Complexity, Chaos, and Change.* San Francisco: Jossey-Bass.

Frei, Frances. "How to Build (and Rebuild) Trust." TED2018, April 2018. https://www.ted.com/talks/frances_frei_how_to_build_and_rebuild_trust?language=en.

Friedman, Edwin H. 2007. *Failure of Nerve: Leadership in the Age of the Quick Fix.* New York: Church Publishing, Inc.

Giguere, Miriam. 2014. "Tolerating Ambiguity—Being OK with Not Knowing." TEDxSoleburySchool, May 18.

Giles, Sunnie. 2018. "How to Fail Faster—and Why You Should." *Forbes*, April 30. Retrieved on February 17, 2018 from: https://www.forbes.com/sites/sunniegiles/2018/04/30/how-to-fail-faster-and-why-you-should/#44d85d1cc177.

Gino, Francesca. 2018. "The Business Case for Curiosity." *Harvard Business Review*, September–October: 14.

Gladwell, Malcolm. 2005. *Blink: The Power of Thinking without Thinking.* New York: Little, Brown, and Company.

———. 2008. *Outliers: The Story of Success.* New York: Little, Brown.

Glaser, Judith. 2014. *Conversational Intelligence: How Great Leaders Build Trust and Get Extraordinary Results.* Milton Park, Abington, Oxon, OX: Bibliomotion.inc.

Goldsmith, Marshall, and Mark Reiter. 2007. *What Got You Here Won't Get You There.* New York: Hyperion.

Goleman, Daniel. 1995. *Emotional Intelligence: Why It Can Matter More Than IQ.* New York: Bantam Doubleday Dell Publishing Group.

———. 1998. *Working with Emotional Intelligence.* New York: Bantam.

Goleman, Daniel, Richard Boyatzis, and Annie McKee. 2002. *Primal Leadership: Realizing the Power of Emotional Intelligence.* Boston: Harvard Business School Press.

Govindarajan, Vijay, and Chris Trimble. 2010. *The Other Side of Innovation: Solving the Execution Challenge.* Boston: Harvard Business School Press.

Grimshaw, Jeff, and Gregg Baron. 2010. *Leadership without Excuses: How to Create Accountability and High Performance (Instead of Just Talking about It).* New York: McGraw-Hill.

Gross, Bertram M. 1964. *The Managing of Organizations: The Administrative Struggle*. New York: Free Press of Glencoe.

Guide to Senior Executive Service Qualifications. 2012. September. U.S. Office of Personnel Management. Retrieved from https://www.opm.gov/policy-data-oversight/senior-executive-service/reference-materials/guidetosesquals_2010.pdf.

Harris, Russ. 2013. *Getting Unstuck in ACT. A Clinician's Guide to Overcoming Common Obstacles in Acceptance and Commitment Therapy*. Oakland, CA: New Harbinger Publications, Inc.

Harter, Jim. 2018. *Employee Engagement on the Rise in the U.S*. Gallup News. August 26. Retrieved from http://news.gallup.com/poll/241649/employee-engagement-rise.aspx.

Harvard Business School Press. 2010. *Thinking Strategically: Expert Solutions to Everyday Challenges*. Boston: Harvard Business School Press.

Heath, Chip, and Dan Heath. 2010. *Switch: How to Change Things When Change is Hard*. New York: Random House.

———. 2013. *Decisive: How to Make Better Choices in Life and Work*. New York: Random House.

———. 2017. *The Power of Moments*. New York: Simon and Schuster.

Hoppe, Michael H. 2006. *Active Listening: Improve Your Ability to Listen and Lead*. Greensboro: CCL Press Publications.

Horsager, David. 2009. *The Trust Edge: How Top Leaders Gain Faster Results, Deeper Relationships, and a Stronger Bottom Line*. New York: Free Press/Simon and Schuster.

Horwath, Rich. 2009. *Deep Dive. The Proven Method for Building Strategy, Focusing Your Resources, and Taking Smart Action*. Austin, TX: Greenleaf Book Group Press.

Hurley, Robert F. 2006. "The Decision to Trust." *Harvard Business Review*, September.

Isaacs, William. 1999. *Dialogue and the Art of Thinking Together*. New York: Doubleday.

Jabr, Ferris. 2012. "Does Self-Awareness Require a Complex Brain?" *Scientific American*, August 22. Retrieved from https://blogs.scientificamerican.com/brainwaves/does-self-awareness-require-a-complex-brain/.

Joiner, William B., and Stephen A. Josephs. 2007. *Leadership Agility: Five Levels of Mastery for Anticipating and Initiating Change*. San Francisco: Jossey-Bass.

Jones, Dewitt. 1999. *Everyday Creativity* (video). St. Paul, MN: Star Thrower Distribution.

Kahneman, Daniel. 2011. *Thinking Fast and Slow*. New York: Farrar, Straus, and Giroux.

Kirton, Michael. 2003. *Adaption-Innovation in the Context of Diversity and Change*. London: Routledge.

Knight, Mary. 2013. "Three Strategies for Making Employee Engagement Stick." *Gallup Business Journal*. Retrieved from http://businessjournal.gallup.com/content/159851/three-strategies-making-employee-engagement-stick.aspx.

Kofman, Fred. 2006. *Conscious Business: How to Build Value through Value.* Boulder, CO: Sounds True.

Kouzes, James M., and Barry Posner. 2003. *Encouraging the Heart: A Leader's Guide to Rewarding and Recognizing Others.* Hoboken, NJ: John Wiley and Sons, Inc.

———. 2011. *Credibility: How Leaders Gain and Lose It, Why People Demand It.* Hoboken, NJ: John Wiley and Sons, Inc.

———. 2017. *The Leadership Challenge.* 6th ed. Hoboken, NJ: John Wiley and Sons, Inc.

Kznaric, Roman. 2013. "The Ancient Greeks: 6 Words for Love (And Why Knowing Them Can Change Your Life)." *Yes!* March 9. Retrieved from https://www.yesmagazine.org/happiness/the-ancient-greeks-6-words-for-love-and-why-knowing-them-can-change-your-life.

Lamott, A. 2013. *Stitches. A Handbook on Meaning, Hope, and Repair.* New York: Penguin Group.

Lee, Guss, and Diane Elliott-Lee. 2006. *Courage: The Backbone of Leadership.* San Francisco: Jossey-Bass.

Lencioni, Patrick. 2002. *The Five Dysfunctions of a Team: A Leadership Fable.* San Francisco: Jossey-Bass.

———. 2005. *Overcoming the Five Dysfunctions of a Team: A Field Guide for Leaders, Managers, and Facilitators.* San Francisco: Jossey-Bass.

———. 2005. *Death by Meeting: A Leadership Fable about Solving the Most Painful Problem in Business.* San Francisco: Jossey-Bass.

Leonard, George. 1992. *Mastery: The Keys to Success and Long-Term Fulfillment.* New York: Penguin Group, Random House.

Loehr, Jim., and Tony Schwartz. 2003. *The Power of Full Engagement: Managing Energy, Not Time, Is the Key to High Performance and Personal Renewal.* New York: Free Press.

———. 2007. *The Power of Story: Change Your Story, Change Your Destiny in Business and in Life.* New York: Free Press.

———. 2012. *The Only Way to Win: How Building Character Drives Higher Achievement and Greater Fulfillment in Business and Life.* New York: Hyperion.

Markman, Art. 2015. "Is Perspective-Taking a Skill?" *Psychology Today,* October 22. Retrieved from https://www.psychologytoday.com/us/blog/ulterior-motives/201510/is-perspective-taking-skill.

McGrath, Rita Gunther, and Ian C. MacMillan. 2000. *The Entrepreneurial Mindset: Strategies for Continuously Creating Opportunities in an Age of Uncertainty.* Cambridge, MA: President and Fellows of Harvard College.

McKee, Annie, Richard Boyatzis, and Frances Johnston. 2008. *Becoming a Resonant Leader.* Boston: Harvard Business School Press.

Mikkelsen, Kenneth, and Harold Jarche. 2015. "The Best Leaders Are Constant Learners." *Harvard Business Review*. October 16 issue.

O'Connor, Joseph, and John Seymour. 1993. *Introducing Neuro-Linguistic Programming. Psychological Skills for Understanding and Influencing People*, rev. ed. Hammersmith, London: Aquarian Press.

Olsen, Erica. 2006. *Strategic Planning for Dummies*. Hoboken, NJ: Wiley.

Oshry, Barry. 2007. *Seeing Systems. Unlocking the Mysteries of Organizational Life*. San Francisco: Barrett Kohler Publishers, Inc.

Partnership for Public Service. 2017. *The Best Places to Work in the Federal Government: 2017 Rankings*. Retrieved from FEVS Website: https://www.fedview.opm.gov/2016FILES/2016_FEVS_Technical_Report.pdf.

Patterson, Kerry, Joseph Grenny, Ron McMillan, and Al Switzler. 2002. *Crucial Confrontations: Tools for Resolving Broken Promises, Violated Expectations, and Bad Behavior*. New York: McGraw-Hill.

———. 2005. *Crucial Conversations: Tools for Talking When Stakes Are High*. New York: McGraw-Hill.

Patterson, Kerry, Joseph Grenny, David Maxfield, and Ron McMillan. 2008. *Influencer: The Power to Change Anything*. New York: McGraw-Hill.

Pink, Daniel. 2018. *When: The Scientific Secrets of Perfect Timing*. New York: Penguin Random House LLC.

Quinn, Robert E. 1996. *Deep Change: Discovering the Leader Within*. San Francisco: Jossey-Bass.

———. 2004. *Building the Bridge as You Walk on It: A Guide for Leading Change*. San Francisco: Jossey-Bass.

Rhodes, Ben. 2018. *The World as It Is: A Memoir of the Obama White House*. New York: Random House.

Runde, Craig E., and Tim A. Flanagan. 2010. *Developing Your Conflict Competence*. San Francisco: Jossey-Bass.

———. 2013. *Becoming a Conflict Competent Leader*. 2nd ed. San Francisco: Jossey-Bass.

Senge, Peter. 2006. *The Fifth Discipline: The Art and Practice of the Learning Organization*, rev. ed. New York: Doubleday.

Siebert, Al. 2005. *The Resiliency Advantage: Master Change, Thrive Under Pressure, and Bounce Back from Setbacks*. San Francisco: Berrett-Koehler.

Sinek, Simon. 2009. *Start with Why: How Great Leaders Inspire Everyone to Take Action*. New York: Penguin Group.

———. 2011. "First Why and Then Trust." TEDxMaastricht. https://www.youtube.com/watch?v=4VdO7LuoBzM.

Sloan, Julia. 2006. *Learning to Think Strategically*. Burlington, MA: Elsevier.

Stein, Steven J., and Howard E. Book. 2011. *The EQ Edge: Emotional Intelligence and Your Success*. 3rd ed. San Francisco: Jossey-Bass.

Sugarman, Jeffery, Mark Scullard, and Emma Wilhelm. 2011. *The 8 Dimensions of Leadership: DiSC Strategies for Becoming a Better Leader*. San Francisco: Berrett-Koehler.

Suzuki, Shunryu. 2011. *Zen Mind, Beginner's Mind: Informal Talks on Zen Meditation and Practice*. Boston: Shambala Publications, Inc.

Van Velsor, Ellen, and Jean Brittain Leslie. 1995. "Why Executives Derail: Perspectives across Time and Cultures." *Academy of Management Executive* 9 (4): 62–72.

Walker, Karen Thompson. 2013. "What Fear Can Teach Us." TED 2013. https://www.youtube.com/watch?time_continue=85&v=OwgWkUIm9Gc.

Wetzel, Sloan R. 2007. *Feedback That Works: How to Build and Deliver Your Message*. Greensboro, NC: Center for Creative Leadership.

Wheatley, Margaret. 2007. *Finding Our Way: Leadership for an Uncertain Time*. San Francisco: Barrett Koehler Publications, Inc.

Wheatley, Margaret. 2009. *Turning to One Another: Simple Conversations to Restore Hope to the Future*. 2nd ed. San Francisco: Barrett Koehler Publications, Inc.

Wheatley, Margaret. 2010. *Perseverance*. Provo, UT: www.margaretwheatley.com.

Wiseman, Theresa. 1996. "A Concept Analysis of Empathy." *Journal of Advanced Nursing*, 23: 1162–1167.

Recommended Assessments

Benchmarks 360® (Center for Creative Leadership)
Sixteen skills:

1. Resourcefulness
2. Doing whatever it takes
3. Being a quick study
4. Decisiveness
5. Leading employees
6. Confronting problem employees
7. Participative management
8. Change management
9. Building and mending relationships
10. Compassion and sensitivity
11. Straightforwardness and composure
12. Balance between personal life and work
13. Self-awareness
14. Putting people at ease
15. Differences matter
16. Career management

Change Navigator (Discovery Learning/Multihealth Systems)
An assessment for change leaders that takes participants on a journey through the stages of transition that are common to periods of change and help people to understand and navigate them. Change Navigator is a change process model that has been designed from

the ground up to help individuals accept and support change initiatives faster. It focuses on the emotions of the individuals whose buy-in and support are critical to a project's success.

Change Style Indicator (Discovery Learning/Multihealth Systems)
An assessment designed to measure an individual's preferred style in approaching change and in addressing situations involving change. Three primary styles exist on a continuum: Conserver-Pragmatist-Originator.

Coaching Behaviors Inventory®
Measures three coaching behavior areas (www.davidnoer.com):
  • **assessing**: data gathering, gap analysis, goal-setting, measurement/feedback
  • **challenging**: confronting, focusing/shaping, reframing, empowering/energizing
  • **supporting**: attending, inquiring, reflecting, affirming

Conflict Dynamics Profile® (Center for Conflict Dynamics)
  • Seven constructive responses: perspective taking, creating solutions, expressing emotions, reaching out, reflective thinking, delay responding, and adapting
  • Eight destructive responses: winning, displaying anger, demeaning others, retaliating, avoiding, yielding, hiding emotions, and self-criticizing

Coping and Stress Profile® (Inscape Publishing)
  • Measures your stress level for personal stress and work stress
  • Measures four personal and four work coping resources: problem-solving, communication, closeness, and flexibility

Decision Style Profile® (Discovery Learning/Multihealth Systems)
Measures five decision-making styles and five situational factors impacting decision quality, acceptance, and implementation:
  • Five styles: directing, fact finding, investigating, collaborating, and teaming
  • Five factors: problem clarity, information, commitment, goal agreement, and time

Measures four skills: self-awareness, self-management, social awareness, and relationship management

Everything DiSC Management Profile® (Inscape Publishing)
Focuses on your DiSC management style; directing and delegating; motivating; developing others; and working with your manager. Participants learn about their strengths and challenges as managers and how to adapt to meet the needs of the people they manage—making them more effective managers.

Everything DiSC 363™ for Leaders® (Inscape Publishing)
Eight approaches and twenty-four practices to effective leadership:

1. Pioneering (promoting bold action, stretching the boundaries, finding opportunities)
2. Energizing (showing enthusiasm, building professional networks, rallying people to achieve goals)
3. Affirming (being approachable, acknowledging contributions, creating a positive environment)
4. Inclusive (staying open to input, showing diplomacy, facilitating dialogue)
5. Humble (being fair-minded, showing modesty, maintaining composure)
6. Deliberate (providing a sense of stability, promoting disciplined analysis, communicating with clarity)
7. Resolute (improving methods, speaking up about problems, setting high expectations)
8. Commanding (focusing on results, taking charge, showing confidence)

Everything DiSC Work of Leaders Profile® (Inscape Publishing)
Measures how you approach the most fundamental work of leaders:
- **creating a vision**: exploration, boldness, testing assumptions
- **alignment**: clarity, dialogue, inspiration
- **execution**: momentum, structure, feedback

Everything DiSC Workplace Profile® (Inscape Publishing)
Measures your preferred DiSC behavioral style and identifies your three priorities that shape your workplace experience.
- **DiSC Styles**: dominance, influence, steadiness, and conscientiousness
- **eight priorities**: action, enthusiasm, collaboration, support, stability, accuracy, challenge, and results
- measures your motivators and stressors, how your style reacts to the other styles
- offers strategies for increasing your effectiveness with the other styles and building more effective relationships

EQ-i 2.0 Model of Emotional Intelligence Leadership Report® (Multihealth Systems)
- Four leadership dimensions: authenticity, coaching, insight, and innovation
- Five dimensions and fifteen subscales of EQ:
    1. Self-perception (self-regard, self-actualization, emotional self-awareness)
    2. Self-expression (emotional expression, assertiveness, independence)
    3. Interpersonal (interpersonal relationships, empathy, social responsibility)
    4. Decision-making (problem solving, reality testing, impulse control)
    5. Stress management (flexibility, stress tolerance, optimism)

Five Behaviors of a Cohesive Team® (Inscape Publishing)
A team assessment that measures a team's five behaviors that contribute to building cohesive teams:
1. Trust one another.
2. Engage in conflict around ideas.

3. Commit to decisions.
4. Hold one another accountable.
5. Focus on achieving collective results.

Global Executive Leadership Inventory® (GELI) (Manfred F. R. Kets de Vries, Jossey-Bass)
Twelve dimensions: visioning, empowering, energizing, designing and aligning, rewarding and feedback, team building, outside orientation, global mind-set, tenacity, emotional intelligence, life balance, resilience to stress.

Influence Style Indicator® (Discovery Learning/Multihealth Systems)
Measures five influence preferences: asserting, inspiring, bridging, negotiating and rationalizing.

Kirton Adaption-Innovation® (KAI)
Measures one's approach to problem-solving as either adaptive (step-by-step) or innovative (expansive).

Korn Ferry Leadership Assessment Potential® (KFALP)
A comprehensive assessment for measuring leadership potential. It measures an individual's drivers, experience, awareness, learning agility, leadership traits, capacity, and derailment risks. Norms are applied to provide information relative to leaders who have advanced.

Leadership potential is about what could be at some point in the future, not what is currently. By focusing on measures related to what could be, the tool has been carefully conceived and empirically designed to provide critical data about people—data proven to differentiate those who have successfully advanced from those who have not advanced.

Leadership Practices Inventory® (LPI) (Jossey-Bass/Pfeiffer)
Measures five leadership practices and thirty leadership behaviors, six per practice.

1. **Model the way.**
   - I set a personal example of what I expect of others.
   - the principles and standards I have agreed on.
   - I follow through on the promises and commitments that I make.
   - I ask for feedback on how my actions affect other people's performance.
   - I build consensus around a common set of values for running our organization.
   - I am clear about my philosophy of leadership.
2. **Inspire a shared vision.**
   - I talk about future trends that will influence how our work gets done.
   - I describe a compelling image of what our future could be like.
   - I appeal to others to share an exciting dream of the future.

- I show others how their long-term interests can be realized by enlisting in a common vision.
- I paint the "big picture" of what I aspire to accomplish.
- I speak with genuine conviction about the higher meaning and purpose of our work.

3. **Challenge the process.**
   - I seek out challenging opportunities that test my own skills and abilities.
   - I challenge people to try out new and innovative ways to do their work.
   - I search outside the formal boundaries of my organization for innovative ways to improve what I do.
   - I ask "What can I learn?" when things don't go as expected.
   - I make certain that I set achievable goals, make concrete plans, and establish measurable milestones for the projects and programs that I work on.
   - I experiment and take risks, even when there is a chance of failure.

4. **Enable others to act.**
   - I develop cooperative relationships among the people I work with.
   - I actively listen to diverse points of view.
   - I treat others with dignity and respect.
   - I support the decisions that people make on their own.
   - I give people a great deal of freedom and choice in deciding how to do their work.
   - I ensure that people grow in their jobs by learning new skills and developing themselves.

5. **Encourage the heart.**
   - I praise people for a job well done.
   - I make it a point to let people know about my confidence in their abilities.
   - I make sure that people are creatively rewarded for their contributions to the success of our projects.
   - I publicly recognize people who exemplify commitment to shared values.
   - I find ways to celebrate accomplishments.
   - I give the members of the team lots of appreciation and support for their contributions.

MBTI® Step II (Myers Briggs Company)
The Step II report is an in-depth personalized description of your personality preferences derived from your answers to the Myers-Briggs Type Indicator® instrument. It includes your four-letter type, along with some of the unique ways that you express your type. The MBTI® instrument was developed by Isabel Myers and Katharine Briggs as an application of Carl Jung's theory of psychological types. This theory suggests that we have opposite ways of gaining energy (extraversion or introversion), gathering or becoming aware of information (sensing or intuition), deciding or coming to a conclusion about that information (thinking or feeling), and dealing with the world around us (judging or perceiving).

OPM Leadership 360 (United States Office of Personnel Management)
Measures the fundamental competencies and the five executive core qualifications (ECQs). Retrieved from https://www.opm.gov/policy-data-oversight/data-analysis-documentation/employee-surveys/buy-services/opm-leadership-360/.

- fundamental competencies: public service motivation, integrity/honesty, interpersonal skills, oral communication, written communication, continual learning
- executive core qualifications:
  - **leading change**: creativity and innovation, external awareness, flexibility, resilience, entrepreneurship, problem-solving, technical credibility
  - **business acumen**: financial management, human capital management, technology management
    - **building coalitions**: partnering, political savvy, influencing/negotiating, strategic thinking, vision
    - **leading people**: conflict management, leveraging diversity, developing others, team building
    - **results driven**: accountability, customer service, decisiveness

Political Skill Inventory® (Ferris, Davidson, and Perrewe 2005)
Measures four dimensions of political skill: social astuteness, interpersonal influence, networking ability, and apparent sincerity.

Political Savvy Assessment® (Brandon Partners)
Measures the following strategies:

- **character strategies**: personal integrity, performance integrity
- **awareness strategies**: knows the corporate buzz, studies politics, savvy attitudes
- **proactive strategies**: manages perceptions, essential networking, balanced self-promotion, enhances power image, savvy communication, ethical lobbying
- **protective strategies**: detects deception, handles sabotage

Strengths Finder 2.0® (Gallup)
Identifies a person's unique sequence of thirty-four themes of talent and shows people how to succeed by developing them into CliftonStrengths.

Styles and Climates Survey® (Korn Ferry)
This assessment consists of two 180-degree online assessment tools. Together, they give you a picture of the leadership style you use and a revealing view of the impact this has on your team. The six leadership styles assessed are: directive, visionary, affiliative, participative, pacesetting, and coaching. The six organizational climates assessed are: clarity, rewards, standards, responsibility, flexibility, team commitment.

viaEDGE® (Korn Ferry)
A self-assessment to provide insight into learning agility and assist in determining potential. It provides scores on five dimensions: mental agility, people agility, change agility, results agility, and self-awareness, and on overall learning agility.

Appendix

1. Seven Practices Good Leaders Master
2. Seven Practices Good Leaders Master: Derailment Themes Checklist
3. OPM ECQs and Leadership Competencies
4. Crosswalk: Seven Practices Good Leaders Master and OPM ECQs and Competencies
5. Crosswalk: Seven Practices Good Leaders Master and OPM Competencies Derailers
6. 2017 OPM Viewpoint Survey Highlight
7. OPM Memorandum: Coaching in the Federal Government
8. International Coach Federation (ICF) Code of Ethics
9. International Coach Federation (ICF) Core Competencies
10. Sample Coaching Agreements

1. Seven Practices Good Leaders Master

PRACTICE ONE: ACTIONABLE TRUST

Actionable trust is the practice of speaking and behaving in ways that extend trust to others, strengthen trust in relationships that need more, and working to rebuild trust in relationships where it's been broken.

Actionable Trust Skills

- *Extending trust* is the act of choosing to speak and act in ways that demonstrate our interest in offering trust to others and our willingness to do so. Making a request of someone is an act of trusting that the other person is willing and able to honor our request. We can also accept a promise or an offer from someone. Our act of acceptance indicates we are trusting that they will follow through with their commitment to us.
- *Strengthening trust* is the act of wisely making requests or accepting offers or promises from someone that adds more responsibilities to the relationship and increases mutual dependencies upon one another's reliability and trustworthiness. It is about balancing risks and rewards.
- *Rebuilding trust* is the act of restoring broken trust. It may take the form of restoring someone else's trust in us when we have broken trust with them; or it may take the form of restoring our trust in someone who has broken trust with us.

PRACTICE TWO: AUTHENTIC ENGAGEMENT

Authentic engagement is the practice of genuinely and authentically connecting with others. It's about dispelling fear and loving one another. It's about creating and fostering a sense of belonging—the belief that we are a part of something bigger than ourselves. And it's about cultivating the courage to be vulnerable and open to joy, compassion, meaning, and purpose.

Authentic Engagement Skills

- *Dispelling fear* is the act of learning to unconsciously and impulsively react less frequently and to consciously and intentionally respond more frequently to strong emotions. It's the act of shifting one's emotional and physiological states from fear and stress to love and relaxation.
- *Fostering belonging* is the act of being who you are; deeply believing in yourself; and courageously sharing your authentic self with others. It's discovering sacredness in both taking a stand when facing the unknown alone and becoming a part of

something bigger than yourself in connection with others who share a belief in something meaningful and purposeful.

- *Cultivating courage* is the act of intentionally choosing to face and embrace our emotions, the things we cannot control, and responding with purposeful action to dispel fear and nurture love. It's developing the mental and moral strength to venture into or withstand dangers or difficulties.

PRACTICE THREE: ALIGNED ACCOUNTABILITY

Aligned accountability is the practice of clarifying standards for yourself and others; holding everyone, including yourself, accountable to the standards; and providing direct feedback.

Aligned Accountability Skills

- *Clarifying standards* is the act of spelling out specific criteria or action steps that one expects of oneself or of another for the successful execution of goals, tasks, or activities.
- *Holding everyone accountable* is the act of consistently holding everyone involved accountable. It's about clarifying expectations, commitments, and responsibilities among all parties. Its purpose is to create consistency and compel action toward mission execution.
- *Providing direct feedback* is the act of directly and clearly providing feedback to another person that clarifies the context in which an event occurred; words that were spoken and actions that were observed; the observer's interpretation of the observed words and actions; and the observer's request for future actions.

PRACTICE FOUR: ADAPTIVE LEARNING AND MASTERY

Adaptive learning and mastery is the practice of embracing curiosity and acknowledging we don't know what we don't know. It's adopting a beginner's mind; embracing curiosity

and improve more quickly.

Adaptive Learning and Mastery Skills

- *Embracing curiosity* is the act of acknowledging we don't know what we don't know. It's about embracing challenges and asking, "What if?"
- *Adopting a beginner's mind* is the act of approaching learning with openness, curiosity, and a vision of new possibilities. It's about accepting not knowing and a willingness to experiment and practice new behaviors to deepen and broaden learning.
- *Failing faster* is the act of shifting one's mind-set from seeing failure as a reflection of one's personal incompetence to a perspective of viewing failure as an opportunity

for new learning. It's approaching failure as an opportunity for gleaning feedback for improvement and new learning.

PRACTICE FIVE: APTLY NAVIGATING COMPLEXITY, CHAOS, AND AMBIGUITY

Aptly navigating complexity, chaos, and ambiguity is the practice of accepting that you don't know all the answers, questions, data, circumstances, barriers, obstacles, or opportunities. It's about building resiliency so that you can bounce back from hardships and challenging circumstances. It's learning to intentionally respond more frequently and to impulsively react less often in the face of complexity, chaos, and ambiguity.

Aptly Navigating Complexity, Chaos, and Ambiguity Skills

- *Accepting "not knowing"* is the act of accepting that we don't know all the answers, questions, facts, possible outcomes, contingencies, barriers, obstacles, or opportunities. It's about willingly embracing the discomfort of ambiguity and beginning to master the process of navigating through the unknown with courage and confidence instead of fear and insecurity.
- *Building resilience* is the act of increasing one's capacity to recover or bounce back from difficulties and challenging circumstances. It's increasing one's ability to be elastic, flexible, and adaptable when facing stressful and demanding events.
- *Responding more, reacting less* is the act of reacting less to fearful emotions and responding more with love. It's about accepting that we don't know all we wish we knew in the midst of complexity, chaos, and ambiguity; and building our resiliency capacity to be elastic, flexible, and adaptable when facing stressful and demanding circumstances.

PRACTICE SIX: ADROITNESS AT STRATEGIC THINKING

Adroitness at strategic thinking is the practice of developing mastery at thinking strategically. First, it's about first knowing your *why*—that is, knowing why you believe what you believe. Second, it's about making quality decisions and incorporating dialogue. Third, it's about learning to juggle competing demands.

Adroitness at Strategic Thinking Skills

- *Knowing your why* is the act of knowing why you believe what you believe and how that belief fuels your sense of purpose and meaning in life and work. Then it's telling your story in a way that communicates your values, strengths, and vision.
- *Making quality decisions* is the act of practicing dialogue to explore alternative viewpoints; exploring for data that challenges our mental models; and recognizing uncertainty, ambiguity, and chaos. It's ensuring that all stakeholders have a place

and a voice at the table. It's creating a sense of personal and shared ownership in the decision-making process.

- *Juggling competing demands* is the act of identifying and juggling competing demands that are critical factors in mission execution. It's learning to prioritize time, effort, and resources. It's learning to be agile and adaptable; being able to realign and reprioritize in the midst of complexity, chaos, and ambiguity.

PRACTICE SEVEN: AUDACIOUS PURSUIT OF MISSION EXECUTION

The practice of learning to connect our actions to strategy, then enabling others to fully engage in mission execution activities and consistently express meaningful recognition for team members' contributions to mission excellence.

Audacious Pursuit of Mission Execution Skills

- *Connecting actions to strategy* is the act of identifying strategic actions that each employee is responsible for carrying out and connecting them with the agency's strategy for mission execution.
- *Enabling action* is the act of putting the right people in the right positions and empowering them to take strategic action aligned with mission execution. It's about building relationships with your people so that you can coach and mentor and guide them in their career development. It's about positioning your people for maximum engagement, contribution, and mission ownership.
- *Giving meaningful recognition* is the act of personalizing and delivering meaningful recognition for an employee's contribution in a way that is meaningful to the recipient. It creates a sense of connection and belonging; a belief that they are a part of something greater than themselves.

2. Seven Practices Good Leaders Master and Derailment Themes and Behaviors Checklist

Seven Practices Good Leaders Master	Derailment Themes*	Derailment Behaviors*
Practice One: **Actionable Trust** ❑ Extend trust. ❑ Strengthen trust. ❑ Rebuild trust.	❑ problems with interpersonal relationships ❑ failure to meet business objectives ❑ inability to change or adapt during a transition	❑ betrayal of trust ❑ does not lead without micromanaging ❑ betrayal of trust ❑ conflict with upper management
Practice Two: **Authentic Engagement** ❑ Dispel fear. ❑ Foster belonging. ❑ Cultivate courage.	❑ problems with interpersonal relationships ❑ inability to change or adapt during a transition	❑ insensitive to others ❑ cold, aloof ❑ arrogant ❑ overly ambitious ❑ authoritarian ❑ poor relationships ❑ organizational isolation ❑ poor working relations ❑ does not treat others with courtesy and respect ❑ does not manage and resolve conflicts effectively ❑ does not respect cultural, religious, gender, and racial differences ❑ does not lead without micromanaging ❑ conflict with upper management ❑ fails to adapt to organizational change ❑ is not open to new ideas and opinions from others

	❏ inability to build and lead a team	❏ inability to build a team ❏ inability to lead a team ❏ does not inspire pride and team spirit among team members ❏ does not build teams of appropriate size and structure to accomplish work goals
Practice Three: Aligned Accountability ❏ Clarify standards. ❏ Hold everyone accountable. ❏ Provide direct feedback.	❏ failure to meet business objectives	❏ poor performance ❏ fails to achieve results within set time frames ❏ lack of follow-through ❏ lack of hard work ❏ overly ambitious
	❏ inability to build and lead a team	❏ inability to build a team ❏ inability to lead a team ❏ failing to staff effectively ❏ can't manage subordinates
Practice Four: Adaptive Learning and Mastery ❏ Embrace curiosity. ❏ Adopt a beginner's mind. ❏ Fail faster.	❏ inability to change or adapt during a transition	❏ unable to develop or adapt ❏ does not recognize his or her strengths and weaknesses ❏ too narrow business experience ❏ narrow functional orientation ❏ not prepared for promotion
	❏ failure to meet business objectives	❏ poor performance
Practice Five: Aptly Navigating Complexity, Chaos, and Ambiguity ❏ Accept "not knowing." ❏ Build resilience. ❏ Respond more, react less.	❏ inability to change or adapt during a transition	❏ unable to adapt to a boss ❏ unable to adapt to a culture ❏ conflict with upper management ❏ strategic differences with management

Practice Six: Adroitness at Strategic Thinking	❑ inability to change or adapt during a transition	❑ unable to adapt to a boss with a different style
❑ First, know your *why*. ❑ Make quality decisions. ❑ Juggle competing demands.		❑ unable to think strategically ❑ difficulty making strategic decisions ❑ unable to adapt to a boss ❑ unable to adapt to a culture ❑ does not make sound and timely decisions
Practice Seven: Audacious Pursuit of Mission Execution	❑ problems with interpersonal relationships	❑ insensitive to others ❑ poor relationships
❑ Connect actions to strategy. ❑ Enable action. ❑ Give meaningful recognition.	❑ inability to build and lead a team	❑ inability to build a team ❑ inability to lead a team ❑ failure to staff effectively
	❑ inability to change or adapt during a transition	❑ strategic differences with management

*Derailment Themes adapted from Table 1, *Themes in Derailment Research* (Van Velsor and Leslie, 1995). Derailment Behaviors adapted from *Themes in Derailment Research* (Van Velsor, and Leslie, 1995), OPM Leadership 360.

3. OPM ECQs and Leadership Competencies

FUNDAMENTAL COMPETENCIES

Public Service Motivation
- shows a commitment to serve the public
- ensures that actions meet public needs
- aligns organizational objectives and practices with public interests

Integrity/Honesty
- behaves in an honest, fair, and ethical manner
- shows consistency in words and actions
- models high standards of ethics

Interpersonal Skills
- treats others with courtesy, sensitivity, and respect
- considers and responds appropriately to the needs and feelings of different people in different situations

Oral Communication
- makes clear and convincing oral presentations
- listens effectively; clarifies information as needed

Written Communication
- writes in a clear, concise, organized, and convincing manner for the intended audience

Continual Learning
- assesses and recognizes own strengths and weaknesses
- pursues self-development

ECQ: LEADING CHANGE

This core qualification involves the ability to bring about strategic change, both within and outside the organization, to meet organizational goals. Inherent to this ECQ is the ability to establish an organizational vision and to implement it in a continuously changing environment.

Creativity and Innovation
- develops new insights into situations
- questions conventional approaches
- encourages new ideas and innovations
- designs and implements new or cutting-edge programs/processes

Vision
- takes a long-term view and builds a shared vision with others
- acts as a catalyst for organizational change
- influences others to translate vision into action

External Awareness
- understands and keeps up-to-date on local, national, and international policies and trends that affect the organization and shape stakeholders' views
- is aware of the organization's impact on the external environment

Flexibility
- is open to change and new information
- rapidly adapts to new information, changing conditions, or unexpected obstacles

Resilience
- deals effectively with pressure
- remains optimistic and persistent, even under adversity
- recovers quickly from setbacks

Strategic Thinking
- formulates objectives and priorities, and implements plans consistent with the long-term interests of the organization in a global environment
- capitalizes on opportunities and manages risks

ECQ: LEADING PEOPLE

This core qualification involves the ability to lead people toward meeting the organization's vision, mission, and goals. Inherent to this ECQ is the ability to provide an inclusive workplace that fosters the development of others, facilitates cooperation and teamwork, and supports constructive resolution of conflicts.

Conflict Management
- encourages creative tension and differences of opinions
- anticipates and takes steps to prevent counterproductive confrontations
- manages and resolves conflicts and disagreements in a constructive manner

Leveraging Diversity
- fosters an inclusive workplace where diversity and individual differences are valued and leveraged to achieve the vision and mission of the organization

Developing Others
- develops the ability of others to perform and contribute to the organization by providing ongoing feedback and by providing opportunities to learn through formal and informal methods

Team Building
- inspires and fosters team commitment, spirit, pride, and trust; facilitates cooperation and motivates team members to accomplish group goals

ECQ: RESULTS DRIVEN

This core qualification involves the ability to meet organizational goals and customer expectations. Inherent to this ECQ is the ability to make decisions that produce high-quality results by applying technical knowledge, analyzing problems, and calculating risks.

Accountability
- holds self and others accountable for measurable high-quality, timely, and cost-effective results
- determines objectives, sets priorities, and delegates work
- accepts responsibility for mistakes
- complies with established control systems and rules

Customer Service
- anticipates and meets the needs of both internal and external customers
- delivers high-quality products and services
- is committed to continuous improvement

Decisiveness
- makes well-informed, effective, and timely decisions, even when data are limited or solutions produce unpleasant consequences
- perceives the impact and implications of decisions

Entrepreneurship
- positions the organization for future success by identifying new opportunities
- builds the organization by developing or improving products or services
- takes calculated risks to accomplish organizational objectives

Problem-Solving
- identifies and analyzes problems
- weighs relevance and accuracy of information
- generates and evaluates alternative solutions
- makes recommendations

Technical Credibility
- understands and appropriately applies principles, procedures, requirements, regulations, and policies related to specialized expertise

ECQ: Business Acumen

This core qualification involves the ability to manage human, financial, and information resources strategically.

Financial Management
- understands the organization's processes
- prepares, justifies, and administers the program budget
- oversees procurement and contracting to achieve desired results
- monitors expenditures and uses cost-benefit thinking to set priorities

Human Capital Management
- builds and manages workforce based on organizational goals, budget considerations, and staffing needs
- ensures that employees are appropriately recruited, selected, appraised, and rewarded
- takes action to address performance problems
- manages a multisector workforce and a variety of work situations

Technology Management
- keeps up-to-date on technological developments
- makes effective use of technology to achieve results
- ensures access to and security of technology systems

ECQ: Building Coalitions

This core qualification involves the ability to build coalitions internally and with other federal agencies; state and local governments; nonprofit and private sector organizations; foreign governments; or international organizations to achieve common goals.

Partnering
- develops networks and builds alliances
- collaborates across boundaries to build strategic relationships and achieve common goals

Political Savvy
- identifies internal and external politics that impact the work of the organization
- perceives organizational and political reality and acts accordingly

Influencing/Negotiating
- persuades others
- builds consensus through give-and-take
- gains cooperation from others to obtain information and accomplish goals

4. Crosswalk: Seven Practices Good Leaders Master & OPM ECQs and Competencies

OPM ECQs and Competencies	Seven Practices Good Leaders Master
Fundamental Competencies	
Public service motivation—shows a commitment to serve the public; ensures that actions meet public needs; aligns organizational objectives and practices with public interests	**Practice Six: Adroitness at Strategic Thinking** • First, know your *why*.
Integrity/honesty—behaves in an honest, fair, and ethical manner; shows consistency in words and actions; models high standards of ethics	**Practice One: Actionable Trust** • Extend trust. • Strengthen trust. • Rebuild trust.
Interpersonal skills—treats others with courtesy, sensitivity, and respect; considers and responds appropriately to the needs and feelings of different people in different situations	**Practice Two: Authentic Engagement** • Dispel fear. • Foster belonging. • Cultivate courage.
Oral communication—makes clear and convincing oral presentations; listens effectively; clarifies information as needed	**Practice Two: Authentic Engagement** • Foster belonging. **Practice Three: Aligned Accountability** • Provide direct feedback.
Written communication—writes in a clear, concise, organized, and convincing manner for the intended audience	**Practice One: Actionable Trust** • Extend trust. • Strengthen trust. • Rebuild trust.
Continual learning—assesses and recognizes own strengths and weaknesses; pursues self-development.	**Practice Four: Adaptive Learning and Mastery** • Embrace curiosity. • Adopt a beginner's mind. • Fail faster.

ECQ: Leading Change This core qualification involves the ability to bring about strategic change, both within and outside the organization, to meet organizational goals. Inherent to this ECQ is the ability to establish an organizational vision and to implement it in a continuously changing environment.	
Creativity and innovation—develops new insights into situations; questions conventional approaches; encourages new ideas and innovations; designs and implements new or cutting-edge programs/processes	**Practice Four: Adaptive Learning and Mastery** • Embrace curiosity. • Adopt a beginner's mind. • Fail faster.
Vision—takes a long-term view and builds a shared vision with others; acts as a catalyst for organizational change; influences others to translate vision into action	**Practice Six: Adroitness at Strategic Thinking** • First, know your *why*.
External awareness—understands and keeps up-to-date on local, national, and international policies and trends that affect the organization and shape stakeholders' views; is aware of the organization's impact on the external environment	**Practice Seven: Audacious Pursuit of Mission Execution** • Connect actions to strategy. • Enable action.
Flexibility—is open to change and new information; rapidly adapts to new information, changing conditions, or unexpected obstacles	**Practice Five: Aptly Navigating Complexity, Chaos, and Ambiguity** • Accept "not knowing." • Build resilience. • Respond more, react less.
Resilience—deals effectively with pressure; remains optimistic and persistent, even under adversity; recovers quickly from setbacks	**Practice Five: Aptly Navigating Complexity, Chaos, and Ambiguity** • Build resilience.
Strategic thinking—formulates objectives and priorities and implements plans consistent with the long-term interests of the organization in a global environment; capitalizes on opportunities and manages risks	**Practice Six: Adroitness at Strategic Thinking** • First, know your *why*. • Make quality decisions. • Juggle competing demands.

ECQ: Leading People This core qualification involves the ability to lead people toward meeting the organization's vision, mission, and goals. Inherent to this ECQ is the ability to provide an inclusive workplace that fosters the development of others, facilitates cooperation and teamwork, and supports constructive resolution of conflicts.	
Conflict management—encourages creative tension and differences of opinions; anticipates and takes steps to prevent counterproductive confrontations; manages and resolves conflicts and disagreements in a constructive manner	**Practice One: Actionable Trust** • Extend trust. • Strengthen trust. • Rebuild trust.
Leveraging diversity—fosters an inclusive workplace where diversity and individual differences are valued and leveraged to achieve the vision and mission of the organization	**Practice Two: Authentic Engagement** • Dispel fear. • Foster belonging. • Cultivate courage.
Developing others—develops the ability of others to perform and contribute to the organization by providing ongoing feedback and opportunities to learn through formal and informal methods	**Practice Three: Aligned Accountability** • Provide direct feedback.
Team Building—inspires and fosters team commitment, spirit, pride, and trust; facilitates cooperation and motivates team members to accomplish group goals	**Practice Two: Authentic Engagement** • Dispel fear. • Foster belonging.
ECQ: Results Driven This core qualification involves the ability to meet organizational goals and customer expectations. Inherent to this ECQ is the ability to make decisions that produce high-quality results by applying technical knowledge, analyzing problems, and calculating risks.	

Accountability—holds self and others accountable for measurable high-quality, timely, and cost-effective results; determines objectives, sets priorities, and delegates work; accepts responsibility for mistakes; complies with established control systems and rules	**Practice Three: Aligned Accountability** • Clarify standards. • Hold everyone accountable. • Provide direct feedback.
Customer Service—anticipates and meets the needs of both internal and external customers; delivers high-quality products and services; is committed to continuous improvement	**Practice Seven: Audacious Pursuit of Mission Execution** • Connect actions to strategy. • Enable action.
Decisiveness—makes well-informed, effective, and timely decisions, even when data are limited or solutions produce unpleasant consequences; perceives the impact and implications of decisions	**Practice Six: Adroitness at Strategic Thinking** • Make quality decisions.
Entrepreneurship—positions the organization for future success by identifying new opportunities; builds the organization by developing or improving products or services; takes calculated risks to accomplish organizational objectives	**Practice Seven: Audacious Pursuit of Mission Execution** • Connect actions to strategy. • Enable action.
Problem-solving—identifies and analyzes problems; weighs relevance and accuracy of information; generates and evaluates alternative solutions; makes recommendations	**Practice Six: Adroitness at Strategic Thinking** • Make quality decisions. • Juggle competing demands.
Technical credibility—understands and appropriately applies principles, procedures, requirements, regulations, and policies related to specialized expertise	**Practice One: Actionable Trust** • Extend trust. • Strengthen trust. • Rebuild trust.
ECQ: Business Acumen This core qualification involves the ability to manage human, financial, and information resources strategically.	
*Financial management—understands the organization's processes; prepares, justifies, and administers the program budget; oversees procurement and contracting to achieve desired results; monitors expenditures and uses cost-benefit thinking to set priorities	

Human capital management—builds and manages workforce based on organizational goals, budget considerations, and staffing needs; ensures that employees are appropriately recruited, selected, appraised, and rewarded; takes action to address performance problems; manages a multisector workforce and a variety of work situations	**Practice Three: Aligned Accountability** • Clarify standards. • Hold everyone accountable.
*Technology management— keeps up-to-date on technological developments; makes effective use of technology to achieve results; ensures access to and security of technology systems	
ECQ: Building Coalitions This core qualification involves the ability to build coalitions internally and with other federal agencies, state and local governments, nonprofit and private sector organizations, foreign governments, or international organizations to achieve common goals.	
Partnering—develops networks and builds alliances; collaborates across boundaries to build strategic relationships and achieve common goals	**Practice Two: Authentic Engagement** • Dispel fear. • Foster belonging. • Cultivate courage.
Political savvy—identifies internal and external politics that impact the work of the organization; perceives organizational and political reality and acts accordingly	**Practice Two: Authentic Engagement** • Foster belonging.
Influencing/negotiating—persuades others; builds consensus through give-and-take; gains cooperation from others to obtain information and accomplish goals	**Practice Two: Authentic Engagement** • Dispel fear. • Foster belonging. • Cultivate courage.

*These are not leadership competencies, no cross-map to Seven Practices Good Leaders Master.

5. Crosswalk: Seven Practices Good Leaders Master and OPM Competencies Derailers

Seven Practices Good Leaders Master	OPM ECQs and Leadership Competencies Derailers
Practice One: Actionable Trust • Extend trust. • Strengthen trust. • Rebuild trust.	**Fundamental Competencies** *Interpersonal Skills* • treats others with courtesy and respect
Practice Two: Authentic Engagement • Dispel fear. • Foster belonging. • Cultivate courage.	**Fundamental Competencies** *Interpersonal Skills* • treats others with courtesy and respect **ECQ: Leading People** *Conflict Management* • manages and resolves conflicts effectively *Leveraging Diversity* • respects cultural, religious, gender, and racial differences *Team Building* • inspires pride and team spirit among team members • builds teams of appropriate size and structure to accomplish work goals
Practice Three: Aligned Accountability • Clarify standards. • Hold everyone accountable. • Provide direct feedback	**ECQ: Results Driven** *Accountability* • achieves results within set time frames
Practice Four: Adaptive Learning and Mastery • Embrace curiosity. • Adopt a beginner's mind. • Fail faster.	**Fundamental Competencies** *Continual Learning* • learns from mistakes **Organizational Impact** • recognizes his or her strengths and weaknesses

Practice Five: Aptly Navigating Complexity, Chaos, and Ambiguity • Accept "not knowing." • Build resilience. • Respond more, react less.	**ECQ: Leading People** *Conflict Management* • manages and resolves conflicts effectively **ECQ: Leading Change** *Flexibility* • adapts to organizational change • is open to new ideas and opinions from others
Practice Six: Adroitness at Strategic Thinking • First, know your *why*. • Make quality decisions. • Juggle competing demands.	**ECQ: Results Driven** *Decisiveness* • makes sound and timely decisions
Practice Seven: Audacious Pursuit of Mission Execution • Connect actions to strategy. • Enable action. • Give meaningful recognition.	**Organizational Impact** • leads without micromanaging

6. 2017 OPM Viewpoint Survey Highlights

The 2017 OPM Viewpoint survey shows the following government wide results:

This year more than 485,000 employees participated in the FEVS, showing their commitment to improving the Federal government. Employee feedback builds upon and supports agency improvement efforts while providing an important baseline for new initiatives.

I am pleased to report that overall 2017 Governmentwide FEVS results show that Federal employees have a positive perspective of their workplaces. Overall Employee Engagement is at 67, the highest level since 2011. The New IQ (the Diversity and Inclusion index) is at 60, the highest level since the index was first reported.

Across the core FEVS items, nearly 100% remained the same or increased from last year, with the largest increases found in supervisory relationships, management communication among work units, and organizational satisfaction. The highest positively rated items continue to highlight employees' perceptions from last year, including willingness to exert extra effort to get the job done, looking for ways to do a job better, and a belief that their work is important.

While 2017 FEVS results are very positive, survey responses also show several key aspects of Federal workplaces could be improved. Based on employee perspectives, agencies would be more effective to the extent that leaders are able to address insufficient resources, recruit for the right skills, recognize employee performance, and generate commitment and motivation in the workforce.

—Kathleen M. McGettigan, Acting Director,
U.S. Office of Personnel Management, p. 2,
2017 Federal Employee Viewpoint Survey
Governmentwide Management Report.

HIGHLIGHTS FROM 2017 OPM VIEWPOINT SURVEY

My Work Experience

4.	My work gives me a feeling of personal accomplishment.	72%
6.	I know what is expected of me on the job.	80%
11.	My talents are well used in the workplace.	60%
12.	I know how my work relates to the agency's goals and priorities.	84%
16.	I am held accountable for achieving results.	83%

My Work Unit

23. In my work unit, steps are taken to deal with a poor performer who cannot or will not improve. 31%

24. In my work unit, differences in performance are recognized in a meaningful way. 36%

My Agency

30. Employees have a feeling of personal empowerment with respect to work processes. 47%

32. Creativity and innovation are rewarded. 41%

33. Pay raises depend on how well employees perform their jobs. 25%

My Supervisor

46. My supervisor provides me with constructive suggestions to improve my job performance. 64%

48. My supervisor listens to what I have to say. 78%

49. My supervisor treats me with respect. 82%

51. I have trust and confidence in my supervisor. 69%

Leadership

54. My organization's senior leaders maintain high standards of honesty and integrity. 54%

56. Managers communicate the goals and priorities of the organization. 62%

57. Managers review and evaluate the organization's progress toward meeting its goals and objectives. 62%

58. Managers promote communication among different work units (for example, about projects, goals, needed resources). 55%

59. Managers support collaboration across work units to accomplish work objectives. 59%

61. I have a high level of respect for my organization's senior leaders. 56%

Retrieved on February 13, 2019, from: https://www.opm.gov/fevs/reports/governmentwide-reports/governmentwide-management-report/governmentwide-report/2017/2017-governmentwide-management-report.pdf.

7. OPM Memorandum: Coaching in the Federal Government

Monday, September 10, 2018

MEMORANDUM FOR:
CHIEF HUMAN CAPITAL OFFICERS

From:
DR. JEFF T.H. PON, DIRECTOR

Subject:
Coaching in the Federal Government

The U.S. Office of Personnel Management (OPM) is pleased to highlight to Federal agencies the importance of creating a coaching culture. Coaching is a critical tool as the Federal Government strives to develop a workforce that supports the effective and efficient mission achievement and improved services to the American people. The benefits of coaching individuals and teams include higher engagement, retention, organizational performance and productivity; increased focus on mission and organizational objectives; improved creativity, learning, and knowledge; and better relationships between people and departments[1]. The field and practice of coaching is broad, and contains many facets which will require more specific guidance. This memorandum and attached Frequently Asked Questions provides guidance to Federal agencies as they plan, design, and implement coaching activities and programs.

It is important to acknowledge two aspects of coaching:

- Coaching is a sanctioned learning and development activity as described in 5 Code of Federal Regulations (CFR) 410.203. Coaching is one of the most effective learning and development activities for supervisors, managers, and executives. Equipping leaders with coaching skills is a proven and effective way to enhance employee development and performance[2].
- Coaching within the Federal Government is appropriate for learning and development purposes only, and requires the voluntary participation of the individual or team being coached. Coaching is not appropriate as a mandatory requirement for poor performance or in lieu of supervisory performance management responsibilities. Participation in coaching activities, in any capacity, should be included in an employee's Individual Development Plan (IDP).

As agencies develop and implement a coaching program, please consider that creating a coaching culture requires a multi-pronged approach, which includes:

- Embed coaching in your leadership programs for targeted populations (e.g., Senior Executive Service (SES) Onboarding programs, new supervisors training programs);
- Developing internal coach capacity to support coaching for all employees, including individual contributors;
- Leveraging external coaches;
- Developing coaching skills in supervisors, managers, and executives; and
- Implementing peer coaching.

Your assistance to promote and champion the practice of coaching will ensure the successful use of coaching in your agency and Governmentwide. If your agency wishes to find out more information about coaching, please contact your agency's point of contact, email FederalCoachingNetwork@opm.gov, or Ms. Julie Brill, Manager, Work-Life and Leadership & Executive Development, at Julie.Brill@opm.gov.

Attachment (see 508-conformant PDF below)
cc: Deputy Chief Human Capital Officers
Chief Learning Officers
Human Resources Directors
CIGIE

---

[1]MacKie, D. (2014). The effectiveness of strength based coaching in enhancing full range leadership development: a controlled study. Consulting Psychology Journal: Practice & Research, 66(2), 118-137. doi:10.1037/cpb0000005

[2] Ali, M., Lodhi, S. A., Orangzab, Raza, B., & Ali, W. (2018). Examining the impact of managerial coaching on employee job performance: Mediating role of work engagement, leader-member-exchange quality, job satisfaction, and turnover intentions. Pakistan Journal of Commerce & Social Sciences, 12(1), 253-282.

Retrieved on July 22, 2019, from: https://chcoc.gov/content/coaching-federal-government.

FEDERAL COACHING FREQUENTLY ASKED QUESTIONS

Q. What is coaching?

A. Coaching is defined as "partnering with coachee(s) in a thought-provoking and creative process that inspires them to maximize their personal and professional potential (International Coaching Federation)." It is an experiential development process which facilitates change and growth in both individuals and groups. Through structured dialogue, coaches assist their coachees to see new perspectives and achieve greater clarity about their own thoughts, emotions and actions, and about the people and situations around them. The coachee gives power to the relationship, drives the coaching agenda, and is ultimately responsible for the outcome of the coaching engagement. Coaches apply specific techniques and skills, approaches, and methodologies that enable the coachees to develop their goals and design actions to achieve them.

Coaching is one of the most valuable developmental resources we can offer our workforce, and has been linked to positive outcomes, such as increased productivity, retention, and engagement. A successful coaching engagement promotes and sustains professional growth and competence. Coaching topics and goals in the Federal setting should be aligned with the employee's professional goals and organizational mission.

Q. What is the difference between coaching and mentoring?

A. Like mentoring, coaching is considered a developmental activity, which enables individuals to achieve their full potential. While a mentor provides advice, guidance, and subject-matter expertise, a coach uses a process to mutually define actions for professional development without the coach providing any advice. Furthermore, formal coaching is always predicated on a signed agreement between coach and coachee, stating the ethical standards of confidentiality, voluntariness, and self-determination, including the duration of the coaching agreement and the expectations of both parties. It is important to understand the distinctions between these roles to ensure the appropriate use in the workplace.

Q. Who can coach in Federal government?

A. The following individuals are able to "formally" coach:

Professional Coach: an individual who offers support through an ongoing partnership designed to help coachees maximize their potential in their personal and professional lives. Coaches have formal training and are not required to have any specific coaching credentials or certifications.

- **Internal Federal Coach:** a professional coach who is employed within a Federal agency and provides coaching services to other Federal employees across the Government.
- **External Coach:** a professional coach, who is either self-employed or partners with other professional coaches to form a coaching business.
- **Leaders using coaching skills:** a supervisor, manager, or executive who leverages coaching knowledge, approaches, and techniques in working with his or her employees to build awareness and support positive behavior change.

Q. What are some common issues tackled during a coaching engagement?

A. Individuals may engage in coaching for a variety of reasons related to maximizing performance. Examples of potential coaching objectives include the following:

- Develop leadership skills of technical experts interested in supervisory positions
- Facilitate professional transitions (e.g., transition from non-supervisory to supervisory roles, transition into higher level leadership roles)
- Organize and prioritize professional responsibilities
- Clarify vision, create meaningful goals, and develop achievable action steps
- Facilitate change management
- Achieve professional career goals
- Streamline or identify functional efficiencies
- Solve individual leadership challenges
- Excel in self-awareness and self-management
- Identify core strengths and recognize how best to leverage them
- Gain clarity in purpose and decision-making
- Strengthening leadership competencies

Q. How can a Federal employee find a coach?

A. Each agency has a coaching Point of Contact, typically in the Chief Learning Office or Training and Development Office. Employees should work with their Agency POC to find a suitable coach. Since coaching is a learning and development activity, please complete the SF-182 and obtain supervisory approval.

Q. Are coaching sessions confidential?

A. All information discussed during a coaching engagement is confidential unless the coachee gives explicit permission to share or as required by law. A coaching agreement must include a statement of confidentiality that informs coaches of the limits of confidentiality as it relates to Federal employees. Limits of confidentiality in the Federal government include: a report of an act of fraud, waste or abuse; the revelation of having committed a crime; the threat of harm to self or others; the sharing of information in violation of a security clearance; the report of sexual harassment; the requirement by law or a court order to share particular information.

Q. What ethical standards are expected to be followed for coaching in the Federal government?

A. Federal internal coaches are bound to uphold the basic obligation for public service and the standards for ethical conduct for Federal employees found in 5 Code of Federal Regulations Part 2635. These standards supersede any and all coach-specific code of ethics and must be addressed appropriately in the Coaching Agreement, specifically the limits of confidentiality and conflicts of interest.

Q. Can an internal coach act as a coach to anyone in the Federal government?

A. Internal Federal coaches need to avoid situations where they are coaching individuals that could be in their chain of command. Such instances include:
- Engaging in a coaching relationship as an internal coach with a current direct report
- Engaging in a coaching relationship as an internal coach with someone who will imminently become a direct report
- Engaging in a coaching relationship as an internal coach with a current manager in one's supervisory chain
- Engaging in a coaching relationship as an internal coach with a Federal employee and receiving payment outside of regular salary compensation

Using the Point of Contact for the Federal Coaching Database, information listed below, can aid in accessing coaching services across Federal agencies to help minimize the risk of conflicting interests. Supervisory approval is required for all coaching engagements.

Q. What resources currently exist to help me find a coach in Federal government?

A. Federal Coaching Database: An inventory of current internal Federal coaches, whose services may be shared across agencies at no cost. The database is located on OMB's MAX portal and is accessible only to designated points of contact within each agency. Points of contact are responsible for matching coaches from the database with employees who have expressed an interest in receiving coaching. The database was developed in an effort to help Federal agencies enhance their development efforts while minimizing costs and maximizing impact. Each agency has a coaching Point of Contact, typically in the Chief Learning Office or Training and Development Office. Employees should work with their Agency POC to find a suitable coach through the database.

Q. What record-keeping is required for coaching engagements?

A. Coaching in any capacity is considered professional development as long as the goal of the engagement relates to an organization-related outcome. As with any other authorized development activity, time spent in professional coaching, either as an internal Federal coach or coachee, must be approved by the employee's supervisor with consideration for organizational priorities. Agencies should develop a method for documenting coaching hours as part of their program, and should use the SF-182 to document the developmental activity.

Q. What resources currently exist for those interested in becoming coaches in the Federal government?

A. OPM has a variety of resources that provide support, including:
- **Federal Internal Coach Training Program (FICTP):** Federal employees who want to become a coach might consider using this coach training program. The

FICTP is designated by the International Coach Federation (ICF) as Approved Coach Specific Training Hours (ACSTH). Successful graduates of this program can leverage the program to obtain an ICF Credential. Successful graduates may also seek certification through other certifying organizations.

- **Federal Coaching Network Site**: This site is a collaborative interagency space used to promote the sharing of information and services related to coaching. Coaching program managers tasked with planning, development, and implementation of coaching programs can use the Federal Coaching Network site, on Max.gov (an individual account is required to access this site through Max.gov), to find a repository of information to help develop and manage coaching programs. The site includes:
  - Guidelines, samples, and best practices for planners and developers of coaching programs;
  - Documents and plans for implementation of individual Agency coach training programs; and
  - Research and best practices on the ROI of coaching.
- **Coaching in Government Wiki Page**: Federal employees can find information on this site which provides more details on the potential uses and benefits of coaching. Additionally, resources and best practices on coaching in the Federal and private sectors can be found on this site.

Retrieved on July 22, 2019, from: https://chcoc.gov/content/coaching-federal-government.

8. International Coach Federation (ICF) Code of Ethics

*Code of Ethics

ICF is committed to maintaining and promoting excellence in coaching. Therefore, ICF expects all members and credentialed coaches (coaches, coach mentors, coaching supervisors, coach trainers or students), to adhere to the elements and principles of ethical conduct: to be competent and integrate ICF Core Competencies effectively in their work.

In line with the ICF core values and ICF definition of coaching, the Code of Ethics is designed to provide appropriate guidelines, accountability and enforceable standards of conduct for all ICF Members and ICF Credential-holders, who commit to abiding by the following ICF Code of Ethics:

Part One: Definitions

- Coaching: Coaching is partnering with clients in a thought-provoking and creative process that inspires them to maximize their personal and professional potential.
- ICF Coach: An ICF coach agrees to practice the ICF Core Competencies and pledges accountability to the ICF Code of Ethics.
- Professional Coaching Relationship: A professional coaching relationship exists when coaching includes an agreement (including contracts) that defines the responsibilities of each party.
- Roles in the Coaching Relationship: In order to clarify roles in the coaching relationship it is often necessary to distinguish between the client and the sponsor. In most cases, the client and sponsor are the same person and are therefore jointly referred to as the client. For purposes of identification, however, the ICF defines these roles as follows:
- Client: The "Client/Client" is the person(s) being coached.
- Sponsor: The "sponsor" is the entity (including its representatives) paying for and/or arranging for coaching services to be provided. In all cases, coaching engagement agreements should clearly establish the rights, roles and responsibilities for both the client and sponsor if the client and sponsor are different people.
- Student: The "student" is someone enrolled in a coach training program or working with a coaching supervisor or coach mentor in order to learn the coaching process or enhance and develop their coaching skills.
- Conflict of Interest: A situation in which a coach has a private or personal interest sufficient to appear to influence the objective of his or her official duties as a coach and a professional.

Part Two: The ICF Standards of Ethical Conduct

Section 1: Professional Conduct at Large

As a coach, I:

1) Conduct myself in accordance with the ICF Code of Ethics in all interactions, including coach training, coach mentoring and coach supervisory activities.

2) Commit to take the appropriate action with the coach, trainer, or coach mentor and/or will contact ICF to address any ethics violation or possible breach as soon as I become aware, whether it involves me or others.

3) Communicate and create awareness in others, including organizations, employees, sponsors, coaches and others, who might need to be informed of the responsibilities established by this Code.

4) Refrain from unlawful discrimination in occupational activities, including age, race, gender orientation, ethnicity, sexual orientation, religion, national origin or disability.

5) Make verbal and written statements that are true and accurate about what I offer as a coach, the coaching profession or ICF.

6) Accurately identify my coaching qualifications, expertise, experience, training, certifications and ICF Credentials.

7) Recognize and honor the efforts and contributions of others and only claim ownership of my own material. I understand that violating this standard may leave me subject to legal remedy by a third party.

8) Strive at all times to recognize my personal issues that may impair, conflict with or interfere with my coaching performance or my professional coaching relationships. I will promptly seek the relevant professional assistance and determine the action to be taken, including whether it is appropriate to suspend or terminate my coaching relationship(s) whenever the facts and circumstances necessitate.

9) Recognize that the Code of Ethics applies to my relationship with coaching clients, clients, students, mentees and supervisees.

10) Conduct and report research with competence, honesty and within recognized scientific standards and applicable subject guidelines. My research will be carried out with the necessary consent and approval of those involved, and with an approach that will protect

participants from any potential harm. All research efforts will be performed in a manner that complies with all the applicable laws of the country in which the research is conducted.

11) Maintain, store and dispose of any records, including electronic files and communications, created during my coaching engagements in a manner that promotes confidentiality, security and privacy and complies with any applicable laws and agreements.

12) Use ICF Member contact information (email addresses, telephone numbers, and so on) only in the manner and to the extent authorized by the ICF.

Section 2: Conflicts of Interest

As a coach, I:

13) Seek to be conscious of any conflict or potential conflict of interest, openly disclose any such conflict and offer to remove myself when a conflict arises.

14) Clarify roles for internal coaches, set boundaries and review with stakeholders conflicts of interest that may emerge between coaching and other role functions.

15) Disclose to my client and the sponsor(s) all anticipated compensation from third parties that I may receive for referrals of clients or pay to receive clients.

16) Honor an equitable coach/client relationship, regardless of the form of compensation.

Section 3: Professional Conduct with Clients

As a coach, I:

17) Ethically speak what I know to be true to clients, prospective clients or sponsors about the potential value of the coaching process or of me as a coach.

18) Carefully explain and strive to ensure that, prior to or at the initial meeting, my coaching client and sponsor(s) understand the nature of coaching, the nature and limits of confidentiality, financial arrangements, and any other terms of the coaching agreement.

19) Have a clear coaching service agreement with my clients and sponsor(s) before beginning the coaching relationship and honor this agreement. The agreement shall include the roles, responsibilities and rights of all parties involved.

20) Hold responsibility for being aware of and setting clear, appropriate and culturally sensitive boundaries that govern interactions, physical or otherwise, I may have with my clients or sponsor(s).

21) Avoid any sexual or romantic relationship with current clients or sponsor(s) or students, mentees or supervisees. Further, I will be alert to the possibility of any potential sexual intimacy among the parties including my support staff and/or assistants and will take the appropriate action to address the issue or cancel the engagement in order to provide a safe environment overall.

22) Respect the client's right to terminate the coaching relationship at any point during the process, subject to the provisions of the agreement. I shall remain alert to indications that there is a shift in the value received from the coaching relationship.

23) Encourage the client or sponsor to make a change if I believe the client or sponsor would be better served by another coach or by another resource and suggest my client seek the services of other professionals when deemed necessary or appropriate.

Section 4: Confidentiality/Privacy

As a coach, I:

24) Maintain the strictest levels of confidentiality with all client and sponsor information unless release is required by law.

25) Have a clear agreement about how coaching information will be exchanged among coach, client and sponsor.

26) Have a clear agreement when acting as a coach, coach mentor, coaching supervisor or trainer, with both client and sponsor, student, mentee, or supervisee about the conditions under which confidentiality may not be maintained (e.g., illegal activity, pursuant to valid court order or subpoena; imminent or likely risk of danger to self or to others; etc.) and make sure both client and sponsor, student, mentee, or supervisee voluntarily and knowingly agree in writing to that limit of confidentiality. Where I reasonably believe that because one of the above circumstances is applicable, I may need to inform appropriate authorities.

27) Require all those who work with me in support of my clients to adhere to the ICF Code of Ethics, Number 26, Section 4, Confidentiality and Privacy Standards, and any other sections of the Code of Ethics that might be applicable.

Section 5: Continuing Development

As a coach, I:

28) Commit to the need for continued and ongoing development of my professional skills.

Part Three: The ICF Pledge of Ethics

As an ICF coach, I acknowledge and agree to honor my ethical and legal obligations to my coaching clients and sponsors, colleagues, and to the public at large. I pledge to comply with the ICF Code of Ethics and to practice these standards with those whom I coach, teach, mentor or supervise.

If I breach this Pledge of Ethics or any part of the ICF Code of Ethics, I agree that the ICF in its sole discretion may hold me accountable for so doing. I further agree that my accountability to the ICF for any breach may include sanctions, such as loss of my ICF Membership and/or my ICF Credentials.

(Adopted by the ICF Global Board of Directors, June 2015.)
Retrieved on February 13, 2019, from: https://coachfederation.org/code-of-ethics.
*Reprinted with permission, International Coach Federation.

9. International Coach Federation (ICF) Core Coaching Competencies

*INTERNATIONAL COACH FEDERATION (ICF) CORE COACHING COMPETENCIES

The following eleven core coaching competencies were developed to support greater understanding about the skills and approaches used within today's coaching profession as defined by the International Coach Federation. They will also support you in calibrating the level of alignment between the coach-specific training expected and the training you have experienced.

Finally, these competencies and the ICF definition were used as the foundation for the ICF Coach Knowledge Assessment (CKA). The ICF defines coaching as partnering with clients in a thought-provoking and creative process that inspires them to maximize their personal and professional potential. The Core Competencies are grouped into four clusters according to those that fit together logically based on common ways of looking at the competencies in each group. The groupings and individual competencies are not weighted—they do not represent any kind of priority in that they are all core or critical for any competent coach to demonstrate.

A. Setting the Foundation
1. Meeting Ethical Guidelines and Professional Standards
2. Establishing the Coaching Agreement

B. Cocreating the Relationship
3. Establishing Trust and Intimacy with the Client
4. Coaching Presence

C. Communicating Effectively
5. Active Listening
6. Powerful Questioning
7. Direct Communication

D. Facilitating Learning and Results
8. Creating Awareness
9. Designing Actions
10. Planning and Goal Setting
11. Managing Progress and Accountability

A. Setting the Foundation

1. Meeting Ethical Guidelines and Professional Standards—Understanding of coaching ethics and standards and ability to apply them appropriately in all coaching situations.

1. Understands and exhibits in own behaviors the ICF Code of Ethics (see Code, Part III of ICF Code of Ethics).
2. Understands and follows all ICF Ethical Guidelines.
3. Clearly communicates the distinctions between coaching, consulting, psychotherapy and other support professions.
4. Refers client to another support professional as needed, knowing when this is needed and the available resources.

2. Establishing the Coaching Agreement—Ability to understand what is required in the specific coaching interaction and to come to agreement with the prospective and new client about the coaching process and relationship.

1. Understands and effectively discusses with the client the guidelines and specific parameters of the coaching relationship (e.g., logistics, fees, scheduling, inclusion of others if appropriate).
2. Reaches agreement about what is appropriate in the relationship and what is not, what is and is not being offered, and about the client's and coach's responsibilities.
3. Determines whether there is an effective match between his/her coaching method and the needs of the prospective client.

B. Co-Creating the Relationship

3. Establishing Trust and Intimacy with the Client—Ability to create a safe, supportive environment that produces ongoing mutual respect and trust.

1. Shows genuine concern for the client's welfare and future.
2. Continuously demonstrates personal integrity, honesty and sincerity.
3. Establishes clear agreements and keeps promises.
4. Demonstrates respect for client's perceptions, learning style, personal being.
5. Provides ongoing support for and champions new behaviors and actions, including those involving risk-taking and fear of failure.
6. Asks permission to coach client in sensitive, new areas.

4. Coaching Presence—Ability to be fully conscious and create spontaneous relationship with the client, employing a style that is open, flexible and confident.

1. Is present and flexible during the coaching process, dancing in the moment.
2. Accesses own intuition and trusts one's inner knowing—"goes with the gut."
3. Is open to not knowing and takes risks.
4. Sees many ways to work with the client and chooses in the moment what is most effective.
5. Uses humor effectively to create lightness and energy.

6. Confidently shifts perspectives and experiments with new possibilities for own action.
7. Demonstrates confidence in working with strong emotions and can self-manage and not be overpowered or enmeshed by client's emotions.

C. COMMUNICATING EFFECTIVELY

5. Active Listening—Ability to focus completely on what the client is saying and is not saying, to understand the meaning of what is said in the context of the client's desires, and to support client self-expression.
1. Attends to the client and the client's agenda and not to the coach's agenda for the client.
2. Hears the client's concerns, goals, values and beliefs about what is and is not possible.
3. Distinguishes between the words, the tone of voice, and the body language.
4. Summarizes, paraphrases, reiterates, and mirrors back what client has said to ensure clarity and understanding.
5. Encourages, accepts, explores and reinforces the client's expression of feelings, perceptions, concerns, beliefs, suggestions, etc.
6. Integrates and builds on client's ideas and suggestions.
7. "Bottom-lines" or understands the essence of the client's communication and helps the client get there rather than engaging in long, descriptive stories.
8. Allows the client to vent or "clear" the situation without judgment or attachment in order to move on to next steps.

6. Powerful Questioning—Ability to ask questions that reveal the information needed for maximum benefit to the coaching relationship and the client.
1. Asks questions that reflect active listening and an understanding of the client's perspective.
2. Asks questions that evoke discovery, insight, commitment or action (e.g., those that challenge the client's assumptions).
3. Asks open-ended questions that create greater clarity, possibility or new learning.
4. Asks questions that move the client toward what they desire, not questions that ask for the client to justify or look backward.

7. Direct Communication—Ability to communicate effectively during coaching sessions, and to use language that has the greatest positive impact on the client.
1. Is clear, articulate and direct in sharing and providing feedback.
2. Reframes and articulates to help the client understand from another perspective what he/she wants or is uncertain about.
3. Clearly states coaching objectives, meeting agenda, and purpose of techniques or exercises.
4. Uses language appropriate and respectful to the client (e.g., non-sexist, non-racist, non-technical, non-jargon).
5. Uses metaphor and analogy to help to illustrate a point or paint a verbal picture.

D. Facilitating Learning and Results

8. Creating Awareness—Ability to integrate and accurately evaluate multiple sources of information and to make interpretations that help the client to gain awareness and thereby achieve agreed-upon results.

1. Goes beyond what is said in assessing client's concerns, not getting hooked by the client's description.
2. Invokes inquiry for greater understanding, awareness, and clarity.
3. Identifies for the client his/her underlying concerns; typical and fixed ways of perceiving himself/herself and the world; differences between the facts and the interpretation; and disparities between thoughts, feelings, and action.
4. Helps clients to discover for themselves the new thoughts, beliefs, perceptions, emotions, moods, etc. that strengthen their ability to take action and achieve what is important to them.
5. Communicates broader perspectives to clients and inspires commitment to shift their viewpoints and find new possibilities for action.
6. Helps clients to see the different, interrelated factors that affect them and their behaviors (e.g., thoughts, emotions, body, and background).
7. Expresses insights to clients in ways that are useful and meaningful for the client.
8. Identifies major strengths vs. major areas for learning and growth, and what is most important to address during coaching.
9. Asks the client to distinguish between trivial and significant issues, situational vs. recurring behaviors, when detecting a separation between what is being stated and what is being done.

9. Designing Actions—Ability to create with the client opportunities for ongoing learning, during coaching and in work/life situations, and for taking new actions that will most effectively lead to agreed-upon coaching results.

1. Brainstorms and assists the client to define actions that will enable the client to demonstrate, practice, and deepen new learning.
2. Helps the client to focus on and systematically explore specific concerns and opportunities that are central to agreed-upon coaching goals.
3. Engages the client to explore alternative ideas and solutions, to evaluate options, and to make related decisions.
4. Promotes active experimentation and self-discovery, where the client applies what has been discussed and learned during sessions immediately afterward in his/her work or life setting.
5. Celebrates client successes and capabilities for future growth.
6. Challenges client's assumptions and perspectives to provoke new ideas and find new possibilities for action.
7. Advocates or brings forward points of view that are aligned with client goals and, without attachment, engages the client to consider them.

8. Helps the client "Do It Now" during the coaching session, providing immediate support.
9. Encourages stretches and challenges but also a comfortable pace of learning.

10. Planning and Goal Setting—Ability to develop and maintain an effective coaching plan with the client.
1. Consolidates collected information and establishes a coaching plan and development goals with the client that address concerns and major areas for learning and development.
2. Creates a plan with results that are attainable, measurable, specific, and have target dates.
3. Makes plan adjustments as warranted by the coaching process and by changes in the situation.
4. Helps the client identify and access different resources for learning (e.g., books, other professionals).
5. Identifies and targets early successes that are important to the client.

11. Managing Progress and Accountability—Ability to hold attention on what is important for the client, and to leave responsibility with the client to take action.
1. Clearly requests of the client actions that will move the client toward his/her stated goals.
2. Demonstrates follow-through by asking the client about those actions that the client committed to during the previous session(s).
3. Acknowledges the client for what they have done, not done, learned or become aware of since the previous coaching session(s).
4. Effectively prepares, organizes, and reviews with client information obtained during sessions.
5. Keeps the client on track between sessions by holding attention on the coaching plan and outcomes, agreed-upon courses of action, and topics for future session(s).
6. Focuses on the coaching plan but is also open to adjusting behaviors and actions based on the coaching process and shifts in direction during sessions.
7. Is able to move back and forth between the big picture of where the client is heading, setting a context for what is being discussed and where the client wishes to go.
8. Promotes client's self-discipline and holds the client accountable for what they say they are going to do, for the results of an intended action, or for a specific plan with related time frames.
9. Develops the client's ability to make decisions, address key concerns, and develop himself/herself (to get feedback, to determine priorities and set the pace of learning, to reflect on and learn from experiences).
10. Positively confronts the client with the fact that he/she did not take agreed-upon actions.

Retrieved on February 13, 2019, from: https://coachfederation.org/core-competencies.
*Reprinted with permission, International Coach Federation.

10. Sample Coaching Agreements

EXTERNAL COACH COACHING AGREEMENT IN FEDERAL GOVERNMENT

Agreement of Understanding

I understand and agree that:

I am responsible for my physical, mental, and emotional well-being during my coaching, including my choices and decisions. I am aware that I can choose to cancel this coaching agreement at any time upon thirty (30) calendar days written notice.

"Coaching" is a professional relationship with my coach, designed to assist me in creating/developing personal or professional goals, and a strategy/plan for achieving them.

Coaching is a process that may involve all areas of my life (work, finances, health, relationships, education, and recreation). I acknowledge that deciding how to handle these issues, incorporating coaching into those areas, and implementing my choices is exclusively my responsibility.

Coaching does not involve the diagnosis or treatment of mental disorders as defined by the American Psychiatric Association. I understand that coaching is not a substitute for counseling, psychotherapy, mental health care, or substance-abuse treatment. I will not use it in place of any form of treatment or therapy. If I am currently in therapy, begin therapy while in coaching, or am under the care of a mental health professional, I will consult with my provider regarding the advisability of working with a coach, insuring they are aware of my decision to proceed with coaching. I will sign a release of confidentiality between my mental health care provider and my coach for discussing my coaching actions and alignment with my mental health treatment plan.

Information will be held as confidential unless I state otherwise, in writing, except as required by law, which, in the federal government, includes: a report of an act of fraud, waste or abuse; the revelation of having committed a crime; the threat of harm to self or others; the sharing of information in violation of a security clearance; the report of sexual harassment; and the requirement by law or a court order to share particular information.

Coaching is not to be used as a substitute for professional advice from legal, medical, financial, business, spiritual, or other qualified professionals. I will seek independent professional guidance for these matters. I understand that all decisions in these areas are exclusively mine, and I acknowledge that my decisions and my actions regarding them are my sole responsibility.

Coaching in any capacity is considered professional development as long as the goal of the engagement relates to an organization-related outcome. As with any other authorized development activity, time spent in professional coaching, either as an internal federal coach or coachee, must be approved by my supervisor with consideration for organizational priorities. I will follow my agency's guidelines for such documentation.

| Coach's Signature and Date | Client's Signature and Date |

INTERNAL COACH COACHING AGREEMENT IN FEDERAL GOVERNMENT

Agreement of Understanding

I understand and agree that:

I am responsible for my physical, mental, and emotional well-being during my coaching, including my choices and decisions. I am aware that I can choose to cancel this coaching agreement at any time upon thirty (30) calendar days written notice.

"Coaching" is a professional client relationship I have with my coach, designed to assist me in the creation/development of personal, professional, or business goals, and to develop and carry out a strategy/plan for achieving those goals.

Coaching is a process that may involve all areas of my life (work, finances, health, relationships, education, and recreation). I acknowledge that deciding how to handle these issues, incorporating coaching into those areas, and implementing my choices is exclusively my responsibility.

Coaching does not involve the diagnosis or treatment of mental disorders as defined by the American Psychiatric Association. I understand that coaching is not a substitute for counseling, psychotherapy, mental health care, or substance-abuse treatment. I will not use it in place of any form of treatment or therapy. If I am currently in therapy begin therapy while in coaching, or am under the care of a mental health professional, I will consult with my provider regarding the advisability of working with a coach, insuring they are aware of my decision to proceed with coaching. I will sign a release of confidentiality between my mental health care provider and my coach for discussing my coaching actions and alignment with my mental health treatment plan.

Information will be held as confidential unless I state otherwise, in writing, except as required by law which, in the federal government, includes: a report of an act of fraud, waste or abuse; the revelation of having committed a crime; the threat of harm to self or others; the sharing of information in violation of a security clearance; the report of sexual harassment; and the requirement by law or a court order to share particular information.

Coaching is not to be used as a substitute for professional advice from legal, medical, financial, business, spiritual, or other qualified professionals. I will seek independent professional guidance for these matters. I understand that all decisions in these areas are exclusively mine, and I acknowledge that my decisions and my actions regarding them are my sole responsibility.

Coaching in any capacity is considered professional development as long as the goal of the engagement relates to an organization-related outcome. As with any other authorized development activity, time spent in professional coaching, either as an internal federal coach or coachee, must be approved by my supervisor with consideration for organizational priorities. I will follow my agency's guidelines for such documentation.

Internal federal coaches need to avoid situations where they are coaching individuals that could be in their chain of command. Such instances include the following:

- engaging in a coaching relationship as an internal coach with a current direct report
- engaging in a coaching relationship as an internal coach with someone who will imminently become a direct report
- engaging in a coaching relationship as an internal coach with a current manager in one's supervisory chain
- engaging in a coaching relationship as an internal coach with a federal employee and receiving payment outside of regular salary compensation

---

Coach's Signature and Date   Client's Signature and Date

Author's Bio: John S. Lybarger, PhD, MCC

John has served his public and private sector clients as an organization development consultant, program manager, curriculum designer, facilitator, and executive coach since 1993 through Lybarger & Associates, Inc., in Colorado. Currently, John is a certified mentor coach and certified faculty member for Coaching4Clergy and Coaching4TodaysLeaders, global coach training programs offering ICF-accredited coach training. As a nationally known expert, John is continuously honing his ability to engage learners, increasing their competence at mission execution and creating sustainable results. John strives for opportunities to work with executives from both the public and private sectors, taking what he learns from each engagement and applying it to the next—effectively creating a more results-focused and mission-driven impact.

Throughout his career, John has designed and facilitated courses that have built stronger leaders, created sustainable culture change, and empowered teams. His recent experience has included contract work with a Department of Defense agency, designing and facilitating their senior leadership development program, and with the US Office of Personnel Management's Western Management Development Center, where he has codesigned numerous courses. He has served as a visiting program director leading custom projects for many government agencies, including the Department of the Treasury (US Mint and Internal Revenue Service), Environmental Protection Agency, various Department of Defense agencies, and the Defense Contract Management Agency. Additionally, he has codesigned and facilitated custom courses for the US Army, Social Security Administration, Food Safety and Inspection Services, US Customs and Immigration Services, Department of Justice, Department of Transportation, and the Pacific Leadership Academy.

Supplementing his public sector consulting, John has provided career transition coaching services at McKenzie Scott in Denver. As an adjunct faculty member at Center for Creative Leadership, John provided executive coaching and small group facilitation for clients in 2006–2007. His private sector clients have included Qwest, US West, AT&T Broadband, Bank Boston, the Home Depot, Frito-Lay, and Proctor & Gamble.

Dr. Lybarger's book *Leading Forward: Successful Public Leadership amidst Complexity, Chaos, and Change* was published by Jossey-Bass in 2014. John spent the first thirteen years of his career in progressively responsible leadership roles in the health care and human services sectors in nonprofit and profit organizations. He has held executive positions with P&L accountability for more than $3.5 million and span of control over geographically dispersed operations with more than 120 staff. John's leadership success has armed him with real-world experience that keeps him focused on results-oriented, mission-critical, and engaging organization-development interventions.

John has earned a PhD in psychology, an MBA with a management concentration from California Coast University, and an MS in counseling from California State University at Fullerton. Additionally, he is a Master Certified Coach (MCC, International Coach Federation), Board-Certified Coach (BCC, with specialty designations: Executive/Corporate/Business/Leadership Coach, Personal/Life Coach, Career Coach, and Health and Wellness Coach, Center for Credentialing and Education), Newfield-certified ontological coach (Newfield Network), certified mentor coach (Coaching4TodaysLeaders), certified paralegal (ABA-approved Denver Paralegal Institute), and certified mediator (the Center for Solutions, Denver, Colorado). He is licensed as a marriage and family therapist (MFT, CA) and certified as a national board-certified counselor (NBCC), certified addictions specialist (CAS, American Academy of Healthcare Providers in the Addictive Disorders), and certified senior advisor (CSA, Society of Certified Senior Advisors).

Index

Printed in the United States
By Bookmasters